D0598691

Hand-Dyed
QUILTS

Layers of Love

This quilt was inspired by the women of Gee's Bend, Alabama. I was awed by their determination to create quilts that not only warmed their families but also brought beauty into their everyday lives.

56" x 62"   *Hand-dyed, hand quilted.*

Hand-Dyed
QUILTS

Marquetta Bell-Johnson

STERLING

New York / London
www.sterlingpublishing.com

Prolific Impressions Production Staff:
Editor in Chief: Mickey Baskett
Copy Editor: Phyllis Mueller
Graphics: Dianne Miller, Karen Turpin
Photography: Joel Tressler
Administration: Jim Baskett

Every effort has been made to insure that the information presented is accurate. Since we have no control over physical conditions, individual skills, or chosen tools and products, the publisher disclaims any liability for injuries, losses, untoward results, or any other damages which may result from the use of the information in this book. Thoroughly read the instructions for all products used to complete the projects in this book, paying particular attention to all cautions and warnings shown for that product to ensure their proper and safe use.

No part of this book may be reproduced for commercial purposes in any form without permission by the copyright holder. The written instructions and design patterns in this book are intended for the personal use of the reader and may be reproduced for that purpose only.

STERLING and the distinctive Sterling logo are registered trademarks of
Sterling Publishing Co., Inc.

Library of Congress Cataloging-in-Publication Data

Bell-Johnson, Marquetta.
 Hand-dyed quilts / Marquetta Bell-Johnson.
    p. cm.
 Includes index.
 ISBN-13: 978-1-4027-5265-0
 ISBN-10: 1-4027-5265-2
 1. Patchwork. 2. Dyes and dyeing--Textile fibers. I. Title.
 TT835.B333 2008
 746.46'041--dc22

                              2007036999

2 4 6 8 10 9 7 5 3 1

Published by Sterling Publishing Co., Inc.
387 Park Avenue South, New York, NY 10016
© 2008 by Prolific Impressions, Inc.
Distributed in Canada by Sterling Publishing
c/o Canadian Manda Group, 165 Dufferin Street,
Toronto, Ontario, Canada M6K 3H6
Distributed in the United Kingdom by GMC Distribution Services,
Castle Place, 166 High Street, Lewes, East Sussex, England BN7 1XU
Distributed in Australia by Capricorn Link (Australia) Pty. Ltd.
P.O. Box 704, Windsor, NSW 2756, Australia

Printed in China
All rights reserved

Sterling ISBN-13: 978-1-4027-5265-0
        ISBN-10: 1-4027-5265-2

For information about custom editions, special sales, premium and
corporate purchases, please contact Sterling Special Sales
Department at 800-805-5489 or specialsales@sterlingpublishing.com.

About the Artist

MARQUETTA BELL JOHNSON was born into a family of tailors and quilters where a working knowledge of basic sewing was expected. She learned to quilt by watching and helping her grandmother, Hattie Battle Miles, as she quilted covers for cold winter nights. As Marquetta matured, her quick wit and curious nature led her down many creative paths that eventually led her back to the family legacy of quilting. Fortunately, the skills she learned on that journey gave her an extensive understanding of color, design, and pattern. A self-taught artist with boundless creativity and imagination, she has benefited by the lessons she learned from other surface design artists and quilters.

Marquetta lives and works in Decatur, Georgia as a teaching artist, producing dyed fabrics, quilts, and collectibles. She considers herself a community-minded artist using her creativity to impact the world in a positive way. Marquetta sees every stitch she makes as an act of love with the potential to foster harmony, well-being, and peace.

Special Thanks

Thanks to my Husband and Family for the Love that they all give,

Thanks to my Friends who taught me how to Live,

Thanks to Well Wishers who helped me make it through,

A Special Thanks to Dot Moye who taught me what to do,

Thanks to my Grandma for giving me "The Key,"

Thanks to my Mother for Loving me for me,

Lastly, Thanks to Rasheeda P. Burston, my Help in All Endeavors, for typing, filing, and doing what keeps it all together.

My sincere regards,

Marquetta

Acknowledgements

The Center for Survival Arts, Decatur, Georgia, Rasheeda Parada Burston, Director.

Dorothy Moye of Davis-Moye & Associates, Decatur, Georgia.

Mason Murer Fine Art, Atlanta, Georgia, Mark Karelson, Owner/Director.

VSA Arts of Georgia, Atlanta, Georgia, Elizabeth Labbe-Webb, Executive Director.

The High Museum of Art, Atlanta, Georgia, Virginia Shearer, Associate Chair of Education.

Da Spot, Carrollton, Georgia, Ashanti and Yusef Johnson.

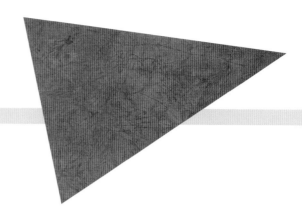

PAGE 126

PAGE 122

PAGE 94

Contents

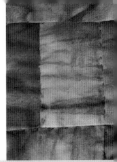

Introduction   8

CHAPTER 1
Learning About Color   12

CHAPTER 2
My Dyeing Method   15
Supplies   16
Preparation   18
Creating Solids & Shades   18
Folded Fabric Dyeing   20
Color Families   28
Drip Painting   44
Masking   46
Dyeing Terminology   47

CHAPTER 3
Quilting Basics   48
Quilting Supplies   49
Basic Techniques   51

CHAPTER 4
Artistic Embellishments   57
Yo-Yos   58
Beading   60
Interfacing Applique   62
Paper Bag Applique   63
Quilting Terminology   64

CHAPTER 5
Projects You Can Make   66
X Marks the Spot Hot Pads   69
Tiny Squares Eye Glass Case   72
Embellished Bars Pin Cushion   74
Nine Patch Pot Holders   78
Beaded Blues Bookmark   80
Triangles & Bars Hot
    or Cold Mat   84
Maverick Block Quilt   86
Hills & Valleys Table Topper   91
Sky & Meadow Floor Pillow   95
House Top Pillow   99
Jazzy Checkerboard Quilt   102
Rail Fence Quilt   106
Blue Blossoms Quilt   111
Color Wheel Checkerboard
    Drop Painted Quilt   116
Appliqued Circles Quilt   119
Shimmering Blocks & Bars
    Table Runner   123
Quarter Square Nine
    Patch Quilt   127
Shadow Block Quilt   130
Come Inside Quilt   135
Quarter Squares & Bars Quilt   138

Metric Conversion Chart   143

Index   143

CREATING BEAUTIFUL TEXTILES has been my passion for over two decades, with hand dyeing, tie dyeing, and shibori as my focus. For many years, I used fiber reactive dyes in immersion and direct application processes. When the opportunity to take dyeing into the classroom and create four hand-dyed and tie-dyed quilts with middle school students was presented to me, I wanted the children to have a good, productive experience without the problems of using powdered dyes, buckets of water, and time-consuming rinsing. In researching an alternative, I discovered that dyeing can be done using diluted air brush colors designed for fabric – proving once again that ingenious ideas are sometimes borne of necessity. As my understanding of this technique grew, I put aside my dye pots and dye powders for the convenience of pigmented mediums.

With this dyeing technique, there are no powdered dyes, caustic chemicals, or rinsing after the dyeing process – just color, visual texture, and immediate gratification. The greatest benefit of dyeing this way is that you need very little water to complete the process. The earth's water resources are not impacted negatively, and you can dye almost anywhere without worrying about disposing of spent dye baths or needing lots of water for repeated rinses.

Yellow Blossom Quilt

Three-dimensional hand appliqued flowers add excitement and visual appeal.
32" x 52"
Hand-dyed, hand appliqued, and hand quilted with beads.

Turn Around & Grow

I often use color opposites like red and green to create dynamic and lively energy in my quilts.
48" x 56"
Hand-dyed, hand appliqued, hand quilted with beads and yo-yos.

Cat Eye Sampler

When I saw my first Cat Eye Block, I immediately set out to create a sampler quilt using variations of the basic block because I love three-dimensional effects in quilts.
64" x 75"
Hand-dyed and hand quilted.

As my use of these alternative dyeing processes in art increased, I found myself dyeing fabric and using it to create quilts and other collectibles – a natural progression because beautiful fabrics call out for sewing. Taking the simple elements of quilting my grandmother shared with me and combining them with hand-dyed fabrics, I have produced work that I believe is uplifting and joyous.

My approach to quilting is spontaneous and improvisational, not based on precision piecing! For instance, I will take a block pattern and change it slightly to create an asymmetrical effect. For me, there is excitement in slight irregularities, and I use them to establish a visual dialogue that is interesting and unpredictable. I use color and design to bring it all together harmoniously.

Continued on next page

Continued from page 9

With hand-dyed fabrics, the interplay of pigments and designs created as the paints move on the fabric provide real visual appeal. When I'm dyeing fabric, my quilt visions are realized as I develop the colors I see in my mind's eye. And having the ability to create unique textiles has brought a definite distinction to my quilts.

It is my sincere desire to empower other quilters to create textiles in an ecologically sensitive way. Water is a precious resource that we must use with discretion. My belief is that you, too, can feel that rush of excitement that comes when the rubber bands are cut from the dyed bundle and colorful designs appear as the fabric unfolds.

My goal in writing this book is to share my step-by-step dyeing methods and quilting techniques in a simple way that could lead to expanded creative horizons for quilters. I hope these examples can help those creating textiles to dye visually interesting, beautiful fabric for use in patchwork and applique.

The projects and quilt patterns in this book are simple enough for the beginning quilter yet engaging enough for those who are more advanced. Helpful tips and conservation ideas appear throughout the book, making the projects less complicated as well as more economical and fun. Sometimes we experience growth when we break out and try a different approach, so feel free to use my suggestions, insights, and ideas as springboards to new discoveries.

Happy Quilting!

Marquetta Bell Johnson

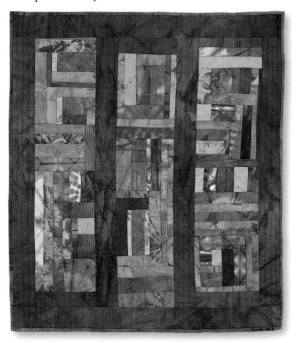

House Top

I am always experimenting with the basic House Top block because you can develop new approaches to make it look altogether different with color placement.
54" x 65"
Hand-dyed and hand quilted

Purple Come Together Quilt

Scraps and strips left over from previous quilting projects become unified and whole as I combine them to create unusual, yet balanced quilt tops.
42" x 48"
Hand-dyed, hand quilted

Upper Regions

English Paper Piecing caught my attention and inspired me to make – totally by hand – this wonderful quilt. It had its debut exhibit at the United Nations.
53" x 82"
Hand-dyed, hand pieced, hand quilted

Yo-Yo Sphere

I was personally challenged to create a round quilt that incorporates yo-yos, buttons, beads; one that would not curl on the edges and would hang beautifully.
42" diameter
Handy-dyed, hand appliquéd with embellished yo-yos.

Spinners

This quilt was inspired by tire rims that spin while the car is not moving. These days almost anything can point to an idea for a quilt.
34" x 58"
Handy-dyed, hand quilted.

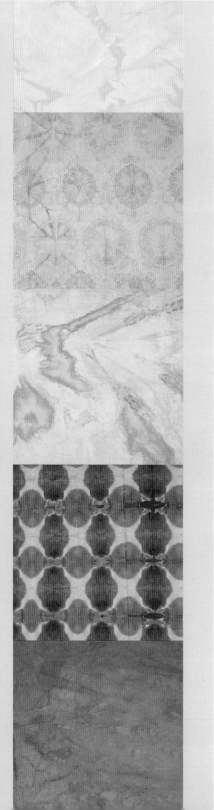

CHAPTER 1

Learning About Color

ONE OF THE FIRST THINGS a quilter must do, once a design has been selected, is to start thinking about color. The information in this chapter will guide you in making color choices to create quilts that are beautiful, harmonious, and attractive. Successful use of color requires observation, experimentation, and a little help from the color wheel, pictured opposite.

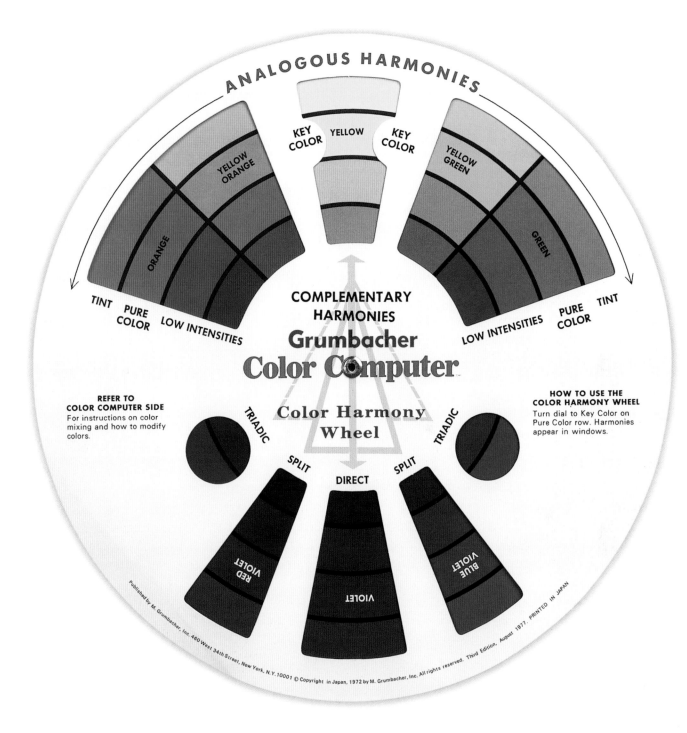

All colors are derived from the three primary colors: red, blue, and yellow. There are three secondary colors: orange, green, and purple. Secondary colors are simple combinations of the primary colors: red + yellow = orange, yellow + blue = green, blue + red = purple. The tertiary colors made by mixing primary and secondary colors, for instance: orange + red = orange-red, green + yellow = yellow-green and purple + blue = blue-violet. You can see other tertiary colors as you move around the color wheel.

Although they are considered to be colors, black, white, and gray are not on the color wheel.

Contrast

As you begin to make your decisions about colors, **contrast** is a major concept that must be considered. Understanding contrast enhances your ability to select fabrics that make your quilts outstanding.

Contrast creates visual interest by expressing difference. There are several ways to achieve contrast; a few of the more common ones used by quilters are: contrast of value, complementary contrast, and warm-cool contrast.

Contrast of value is the difference in color that distinguishes it as a light, medium, or dark fabric. If we make sure to have light, medium, and dark fabrics in a quilt, it clarifies the design and makes depth apparent.

Recognizing contrast of value isn't always easy. To see if you have included enough contrast, select your fabrics for a project, then perform one of these tests:

1. *Squint.* Closing your eyes slightly reduces the amount of light they receive and reduces your perception of color, so contrasting colors become more evident.
2. *Use a reducing tool.* A reducing tool reduces the size of an image, making color less obvious and contrast more apparent when looking at the fabrics.
3. *Photocopy your fabrics.* Make black and white photocopies of swatches of your fabrics. This completely masks the fabric color and brings out its contrast.

Another type of contrast is **complementary contrast**. It is the use of any two complementary colors together. Complementary colors lie opposite each other on the color wheel. When placed right next to each other, the contrast is so strong that the colors seem to vibrate. Strategically separated complements add sparkle and pop to a quilt. The trick is to use them unequally. Let one dominate, and use the other sparingly.

Complementary Colors

Red – Green
Yellow – Violet
Orange – Blue

Finally, there is **warm-cool contrast**. People who study the science of color have proved that colors have a "visual temperature." Some colors are cool (the blues and greens of sky and trees); some are warm (the reds, yellows, and oranges of fire and sun). Cool colors seem to recede or appear as background, while warm colors advance or come forward.

Color or Hue

After contrast, color or hue is another important factor to consider when composing a quilt. Color is subjective – each person has personal color preferences – and color evokes emotion. Here are some tips for using color in quilts:

- Use colors for their emotional appeal. Experiments have shown colors affect our moods. Here are some examples:
  Blue – relaxation, calm, peace
  Red – excitement, passion, strength
  Green – hope, tranquility, balance
  Yellow – thoughtfulness, joy, wealth
  Orange – assertiveness, gregariousness
  Purple – heightened awareness, spiritual growth

- Tones, tints, and shades of colors can be created by adding gray, white, or black, respectively, to pure hues. This adds sophistication to your quilts.

- Analogous color combinations work well because they are so closely related. Analogous colors are the ones that lie next to each other on the color wheel.

- Adding neutral colors such as black, white, gray, beige, and cream to a quilt can give the eyes a place to rest among the other colors.

- Earth tones, such as browns and rust-browns, are all around us and they soothe and comfort. Use them to bring softness to a quilt, to reduce the glaring brilliance of some colors, and make your quilt quieter and more subtle.

Once you have grasped these concepts, it becomes easy to develop interesting color combinations when dyeing fabric.

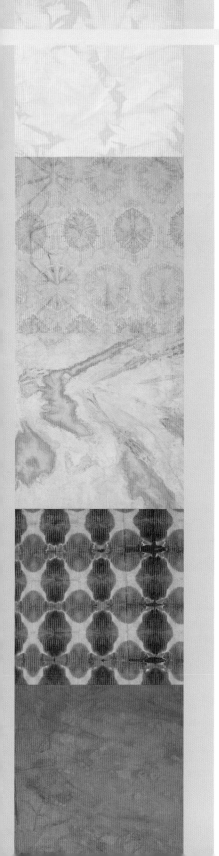

CHAPTER 2

Dyeing Method

THE PROCESS OF DYEING FABRIC with air brush paint is simple and does not involve the use of caustic chemicals or fancy equipment. You need only a few basic supplies – air brush paint, fabric, rubber bands, a plastic container, a squeeze bottle, and water. The process is environmentally friendly because you only need small amounts of water used to mix the solutions, and there's no need for rinsing. You just tie, mix, dye, and dry. No mess and no fuss. This makes it a wonderful process to share with children, and you can dye outside without the risk of harming the environment with toxic chemicals.

You can create interesting textiles by simply pouring the solution onto fabric; however, folding, bunching and tying creates more visual texture. This chapter shows you a variety of techniques for creating dyed fabrics.

Supplies

Air Brush Paint

Using air brush paint for dyeing fabric offers an environmentally friendly alternative to other dyeing methods. You need only small amounts of water to dilute the paint for hand-dyeing (thereby saving natural resources), and you do not need to use any caustic chemicals. The paint is available in a full range of transparent and opaque colors and in pearlized, fluorescent, metallic, and iridescent sheens. Air brush paint comes in a variety of sizes from 2 ounces to 32 ounces and can be purchased in most art supply stores, online, and by mail order.

Air brush paint can be used to color natural fabrics (cotton, silk, rayon, linen, felt, canvas) and on leather, paper, and wood with permanent results. When diluted with water for dyeing, it has a shelf life of three to four weeks for optimum strength. An acrylic product that is considered a pigment, air brush paint coats the fibers of the fabric and migrates through the fibers, but not as easily as dye does, so you have to be sure the paint has saturated all the areas you want to dye. To intensify the color saturation, you can add pure pigments developed by the paint manufacturer.

You can also use air brush paint straight from the bottle, with no dilution, for fabric painting, printing, and stenciling. Air brush colors are waterbased, non-toxic, and meet ASTM-D 4236 Safety Standards. CAUTIONS: **Do not** use around food, and watch out for pets.

Fabrics

Fabrics for Dyeing

Natural fiber fabrics (cotton, rayon, silk, linen, and wool) give the best results. PFD ("prepared for dyeing") fabrics are great to use, too, because they have no sizing or additives such as wrinkle or flame retardants. Check the ends of bolts of white or unbleached cotton fabric for the letters PFD or the words "prepared for dyeing." Another point to remember is that after dyeing and drying, the fabric feels crunchy but it softens after heat setting and handling.

Fabrics for Quilt Backing

If you like you can also hand dye the fabrics that you will need to back each quilt project. Cut the fabric to size, then dye. You could also use coordinating colored fabric. For large projects such as bed quilts, I recommend that you use a coordinating color of a bed sheet.

Tools & Other Supplies

• Plastic basins, 3" to 8" deep, for soaking the fabric in the dye. TIP: Recycle those really tough plastic containers that bulk meats or frozen foods come in.

• Container for warm water. TIP: Recycle a plastic gallon jug to keep water at your fingertips.

• Rubber Bands;

• Disposable vinyl or latex gloves, to protect your hands

• Plastic squeeze bottles

• Various sizes of disposable plastic zipper-top bags

• Newsprint, freezer paper, or disposable plates

• Scissors

• Paper towels, for cleanup

• Drying rack, for air drying

• Iron with a metal soleplate, for heat setting (Nonstick soleplates do not get hot enough.)

Prepare the Fabric

1. Wash the fabric.

The dyeing process begins with washing the fabric with warm water and a mild soap. Pre-washing the fabric is necessary to remove any sizing, oils, or chemicals that might have been used during manufacturing. These substances could interfere with even absorption of the dye solution.

2. Cut the fabric.

After drying and ironing, if needed, I cut the fabric into smaller lengths – about 2 yards is a good length because the process works best on smaller pieces of fabric.

Prepare the Pigment

1. Pour the paint.

Wearing disposable gloves, place the appropriate amount of air brush paint in a squeeze bottle. (Photo 1) Add water. (Photo 2)
Light Color Intensity – 1 part paint to 4 parts water
Medium Color Intensity – 1 part paint to 3 parts water
Deep Color Intensity – 1 part paint to 2 parts water

2. Mix the solution.

Place your finger over the hole in the tip of the bottle and shake well to mix the solution. (Photo 3)

Photo 1 – Pouring paint in a squeeze bottle.

Photo 2 – Adding water to the squeeze bottle.

Photo 3 – Mixing the solution.

Creating Solids & Shades

Here's how to dye a solid-color piece of fabric. The fabric color depends on the intensity of the dye solution. You can also mix air brush paint colors to create custom shades.

1. Put a piece of bunched up, pre-washed fabric in a plastic zipper-top bag. (Photo 4)
2. Slowly pour diluted air brush paint on the fabric, a little at a time. (Photo 5) Pour only enough dye to saturate the bunched fabric, but not so much that you make a puddle in the bottom of the plastic bag.
3. Gently squeeze the paint solution through the fabric, massaging it with your hands. (Photo 6) Close the bag and let it stand overnight.

4. The next day, take the fabric out of the bag and place it – crumpled-up, but not balled-up – on a disposable plate, a piece of unprinted newsprint, or on the paper side of freezer paper. (Photo 7) Let it stay bunched up. The raised areas will dry darker than the flat areas and create a lot of visual texture. TIP: If the fabric is very juicy, place a small piece of un-dyed fabric underneath it to absorb and conserve the solution. Then you will have an extra piece of dyed fabric.

5. When the sample is dry to the touch, hang it up and let it dry completely. It will feel a little stiff, but after heat setting it will soften up.

6. Heat set.

Photo 4 – Putting the bunched fabric in a plastic bag.

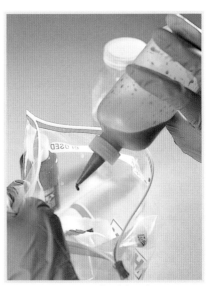

Photo 5 – Pouring the diluted paint on the fabric.

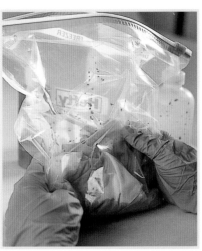

Photo 6 – Squeezing the colorant through the fabric.

Photo 7 – Placing the dyed fabric on a plate to air dry.

Heat Setting

When the dyed fabric is completely dry, it is ready to be heat set. You have two options – ironing and using a clothes dryer.

Heat Setting with an Iron: Heat an iron with a metal soleplate on the highest setting. Using a protective cloth between the iron and the dyed fabric to prevent scorching, iron the fabric on both sides for two minutes.

Heat Setting in the Dryer: Put the fabric in a commercial dryer on the highest setting and tumble for 45 minutes.

 Rinsing Dark-Colored Fabric

Although you do not rinse the fabric when you use this dyeing process, newly dyed dark colors could rub off and stain other fabrics. As a precaution, I wash dark-colored fabrics gently with mild soap and rinse them to eliminate the possibility of having colors rub off on whites and lights in a quilt.

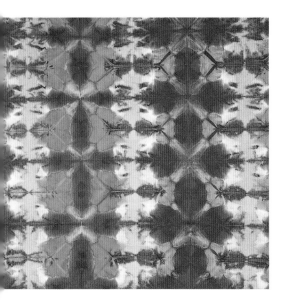

Folded Fabric Dyeing

There are many ways to dye fabric to create random or planned designs. The techniques in this section create pattern and design by encouraging the fabric to resist the dyeing solution in certain areas. Rubber bands are used to secure the fabric after folding because they do not absorb the dye, and they create sharp, defined lines. The rubber bands isolate areas of the fabric from the dye solution strongly or moderately, depending upon how tightly they are applied.

Using the folding and tying methods that follow, it's possible to create many different designs. The way the dye is applied adds interest and makes different random designs. The tying techniques can be used singly or in combination. With a little imagination and experimentation, you'll soon develop your own variations.

Multiple Colors: You can use more than one color to dye each folded piece of fabric. Simply squeeze the colors of your choice randomly on the folded piece. It is best to use no more than three colors for any one fold. It is so much fun to see how the colors blend and combine to create a unique dyed fabric piece.

How to Dye the Folded Fabric:
When you have folded your fabric into bundles and secured it with rubber bands, it is time to dye. Remember to wear gloves to protect your hands and an apron or smock to protect your clothes. Always have paper towels at hand for wiping up minor spills. Work in an area not used for food preparation. Cover your staging area with newspaper.

1. Fold the fabric and secure with rubber bands.
2. Place another small piece of fabric in the bottom of your plastic dyeing container. (Photo 1) (This small piece will absorb excess dye solution and create a coordinating piece of fabric with a mottled, distressed look. This keeps you from wasting dye and it gives you an additional piece of fabric to use.)
3. Place your folded bundle of fabric in the container on top of the small piece. (Photo 2) Remember to **always** wear your gloves.

TIP: Sometimes the surface tension of the fabric can make the dye solution bead up on the tied bundle. Spritzing the fabric with a little water really helps.

4. Place the tip of the squeeze bottle on the bundle, tilt it up, and allow the liquid to seep into the folds. (Photo 3) Hold the tip about ¼" away from the bundle. Dye all areas with your color(s) of choice – including the areas between the folds. Using one to three colors works best. Make sure the tip of the bottle gets between the folds for maximum coverage. (photo 4) The excess dye will seep onto the fabric in the bottom of the container. (Photo 5)
5. Place a small piece of fabric in the bottom of a plastic zipper-top bag. When you have dyed all the areas of the folded bundle, place the bundle in the plastic bag on top of the small piece of fabric. Leave it there overnight.
6. The day after dyeing, take your dyed, folded bundle out of the plastic bag and place it on a disposable plate, on a piece of unprinted newsprint (not newspaper – the ink will rub off), or on the paper side of freezer paper for air drying. When the bundle is slightly dry, cut off the rubber bands (Photo 6) and let it dry some more.
7. When it is almost dry, unfurl your dyed fabric bundle, lay the fabric out flat or hang it up, and let dry completely. (Photo 7)
8. Heat set.

See page 22 for folding and tying techniques

Photo 1. Putting a bed of fabric in the container.

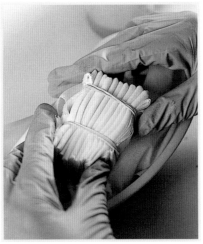

Photo 2. Placing the tied fabric bundle in the container.

Photo 3. Touching the nozzle of the squeeze bottle to the folds of the fabric.

Photo 4. Squeezing dye between the folds.

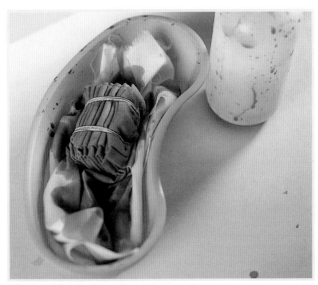

Photo 5. The dyed bundle in the container.

Photo 6. Cutting the rubber bands.

Photo 7. Unfurling the fabric to dry completely.

Fan Fold

1. Fold the fabric piece into thirds. (Photo 1)
2. Place one open end of the folded fabric facing you on a firm surface. Fold up 1" of the fabric, then fold under 1" of the fabric, then fold up 1" – you're making accordion or fan folds. (Photo 2) Continue until all the fabric is folded. (Photo 3)
3. Wrap rubber bands 1" from each end (Photo 4) and one in the middle by stretching the rubber bands over and twisting several times until the rubber bands are tight.

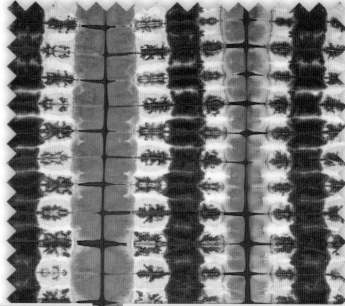

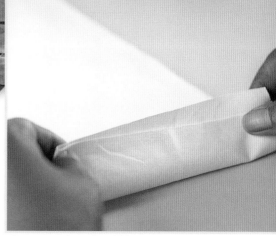

Photo 2. Making fan folds along the short side, folding 1" sections.

Photo 1. Folding the fabric in thirds.

Photo 3. Continuing to make fan folds the length of fabric.

Photo 4. Wrapping rubber bands at each end.

Fan Fold Variation

Additional supplies: Large paper clips

1. Fold the fabric into fourths like the letter "M."
2. Place one open end facing you at a 45-degree angle. Fold up one corner 1", creating a fold at a diagonal. Make 1" fan folds, (Photo 1) putting paper clips on the folded parts to hold them in place as you work your way up the fabric, folding over and under until you finish. (Photo 2)
3. Lay the folded line of fabric on a flat surface with one end facing you. Roll the fabric up on itself until you reach the end. (Photo 3)
4. Place a rubber band around the bundle, stretching it over and twisting several times until the rubber band is tight. (Photo 4)

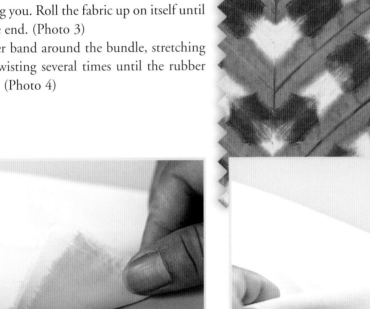

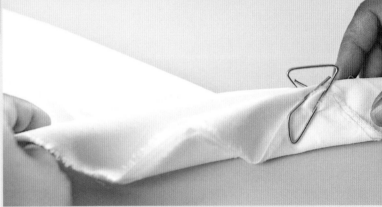

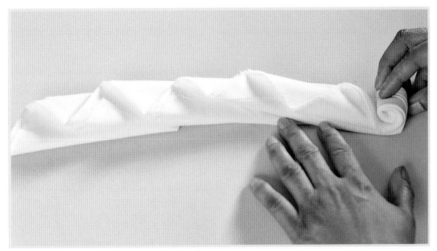

Photo 1. Making fan folds on the diagonal.

Photo 2. Using paper clips to hold fan folds in place until the fan fold is completed.

Photo 3. Rolling the fabric into a cylinder.

Photo 4. Placing a rubber band around cylinder to hold it for dyeing.

Envelope Fold

For this fold, the corners of the folded bundle are tucked in like an envelope. In origami, this is called reverse folding.

1. Fold the fabric into thirds.
2. Place one end facing you on a firm surface. Fold up 1". Fold under 1". Continue, making fan folds, until you reach the end.
3. Put a rubber band on the middle of the bundle to hold it in place.
4. At each end, tuck in the corners of each fold 45 degrees. (Photo 1, Photo 2)
5. Put rubber bands tightly on each end. (Photo 3)

Photo 1. Tucking in the corners at each end.

Photo 2. Notice how the ends are tucked in at a 45-degree angle.

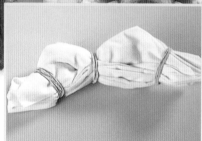

Photo 3. Placing rubber bands tightly on each end.

Checkerboard Fold

Two dye colors must be used to get the checkerboard effect. Dye opposing corners of the folded fabric bundle the same color.

1. Spread out the fabric on a hard surface. Fan fold the fabric, making a fold every 2". Continue until you reach the end.
2. Place the folded fabric with one open (short) end facing you. Fan fold again, every 2" until you reach the other end. (Photo 1)
3. Place one rubber band running from the top to the bottom of the bundle. Place another rubber band running from side to side. (Photo 2)

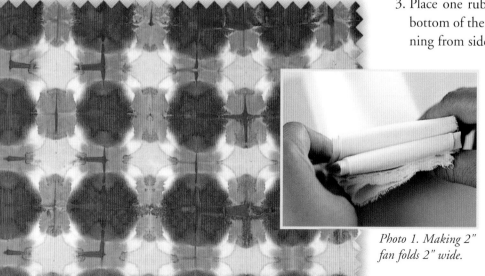

Photo 1. Making 2" fan folds 2" wide.

Photo 2. Rubber bands secure the folds.

Triangle Fold

1. Lay out the fabric on a flat surface. Starting at one side, fan fold the fabric every 2". Continue folding until you reach the other side.
2. Place the folded fabric with one open end facing you. Fold over the end 45 degrees to form a triangle. (Photo 1) Fold straight under, then again at an angle. Continue folding over and under until you reach the end. (It should look like a triangle.)
3. Place rubber bands around 1" from each end of the base of the triangle. (Photo 2) Be careful not to make the rubber bands too tight.

Photo 1. Folding up the corner 45 degrees to form a triangle.

Photo 2. Rubber bands 1" from each end hold the folds in place.

Random Line Fold

1. Lay out the fabric on a flat surface. Starting at one side, with your hands about one foot apart, pinch-fold the fabric towards you, keeping it flat as you pinch it up, until you reach the end. (Photo 1) You can also pinch-fold on the diagonal.
2. Hold the folded fabric up with one hand while you make 3" fan folds from one side. (Photo 2)
3. Fold the bundle in half. Place a rubber band tightly around the middle of the bundle. (Photo 3)

Photo 1. Pinching the fabric into folds.

Photo 2. Fan folding every 3".

Photo 3. The bundle folded in half and secured with rubber bands.

Spiral Fold

1. Lay out the fabric on a firm, flat surface. Pinch a small piece of fabric at the middle. (Photo 1)
2. Keeping the fabric on the surface, twist it clockwise and wind the fabric on itself in a spiral until you reach the end. (Photo 2)
3. Place a rubber band firmly from side to side on the bundle. Place another rubber band from the bottom to the top of the bundle. (Photo 3)

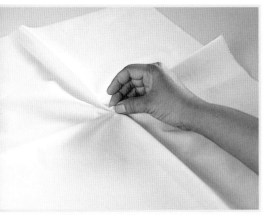

Photo 1. Pinching the fabric in the middle.

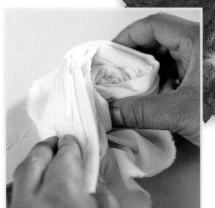

Photo 2. Winding the fabric into a spiral.

Photo 3. Rubber bands hold the folded fabric.

Concentric Circles Fold

1. Lay out the fabric on a firm surface. Pinch a small dab of the fabric at the center with your dominant hand.
2. Pick up the fabric, letting it fall naturally. With your other hand, gather the fabric together. (Photo 1)
3. Place rubber bands along the fabric, starting 1" from the top and at 2" intervals until you reach the end. (Photo 2)

Photo 1. Pinching the fabric at the center and holding up with one hand, while gathering at the bottom with the other hand.

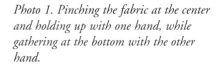

Photo 2. Rubber bands are placed at 2" intervals along length of piece.

Multiple Circle Fold

1. Fold the fabric into fourths so that you have a long strip.
2. About 3" from one end, pinch the edge and scrunch the fabric to create a half circle. (Photo 1)
3. Place a rubber band on the scrunched fabric. (Photo 2)
4. Move to the opposite side. In the middle, create the same circle pattern and place a rubber band on it.
5. Move back to the first side and repeat on the other end, placing rubber bands around the fabric. (Photo 3)

Photo 1. Pinching and gathering at the edge of fold, 3" from bottom.

Photo 2. A rubber band holds the first circle fold.

Photo 3. A fabric piece with three circle folds.

Random Circles

1. Lay out the fabric on a firm surface.
2. Pinch a small area of fabric, pull down around it with your other hand, and secure with a rubber band. Repeat randomly. Vary the size of your pinches for a more random appearance.

Mandala Tie

1. Fold the fabric in half lengthwise. Fold the corners at an angle to the center. Reverse fold in half to create four wedges in a stack. (Photo 1)
2. Gather the tip and put a rubber band on it. Gather a bit of the right side and put a rubber band on it. Do the same for the left side. (Photo 2)

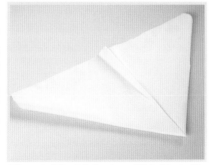

Photo 1. The fabric piece, folded in half with the corners folded to the center.

Photo 2. The tip and each side are gathered and secured with rubber bands.

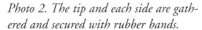

Color Families

Using hand-dyed fabric in my quilts has been very liberating. Whether you use all hand-dyed pieces or use them to complement batiks and printed fabrics, hand-dyed pieces add interest and excitement to art work. Looking at pieces of dyed fabric inspires me and gives me ideas for what to make out of it.

The fabric samples that follow are divided into color families. The caption of each photo includes the air brush paint colors and the tying style. Use this information to develop your own hand-dyed fabric and to gain an understanding of what happens when certain colors in pigment form come together.

Hand-dyed designs can be replicated but they cannot really be exactly duplicated because the process is unique and random. As with anything handmade, a hand-dyed fabric is one of a kind.

Taking It to the Next Level

Not all dyed fabrics turn out as expected or planned. You can have a good air brush paint solution, well-prepared fabric, and excellent tying techniques – all the elements that usually guarantee a successful outcome. However, there will always be slight differences in dye runs. Even if the result you get isn't the one you wanted, do not consider any fabric ugly. Instead, see it as potentially beautiful. Even if it doesn't have an even dispersion of color, you can use the fabric as a background for a little more surface design.

Take a "bland" fabric to another level by painting, printing, or stenciling on it with metallic, opaque, or iridescent paint. Use it as an opportunity to create something unusual. If at first you don't succeed, dye, dye again!

Reds

Red Pure Hue – Solid Hand Dyed   *Red Tint – Solid Hand Dyed*   *Red Shade*

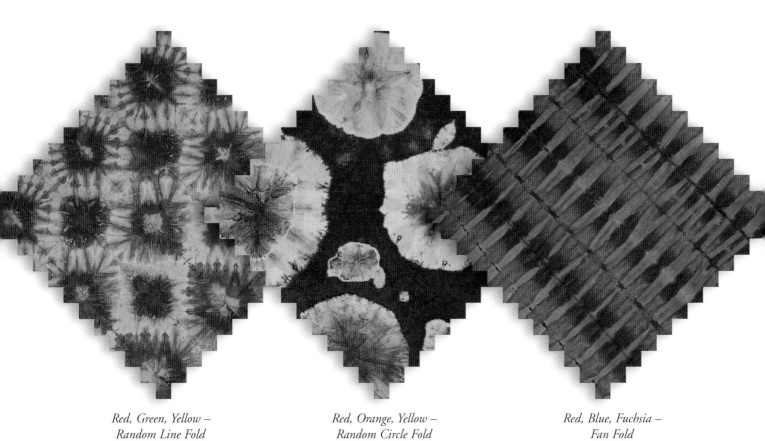

Red, Green, Yellow –
Random Line Fold

Red, Orange, Yellow –
Random Circle Fold

Red, Blue, Fuchsia –
Fan Fold

Red, Yellow, Blue – Mandala Fold

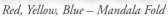

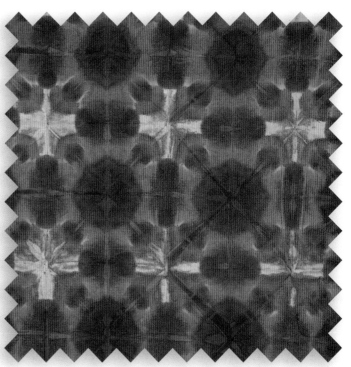

Red, Fuchsia, Yellow – Triangle Fold

Fuchsias

Top to bottom at right:
A – Fuchsia Pure Hue – Solid Hand Dyed
B – Fuchsia Tone – Solid Hand Dyed
C – Fuchsia Shade – Solid Hand Dyed
D – Fuchsia, Blue, Red – Concentric Circle Fold

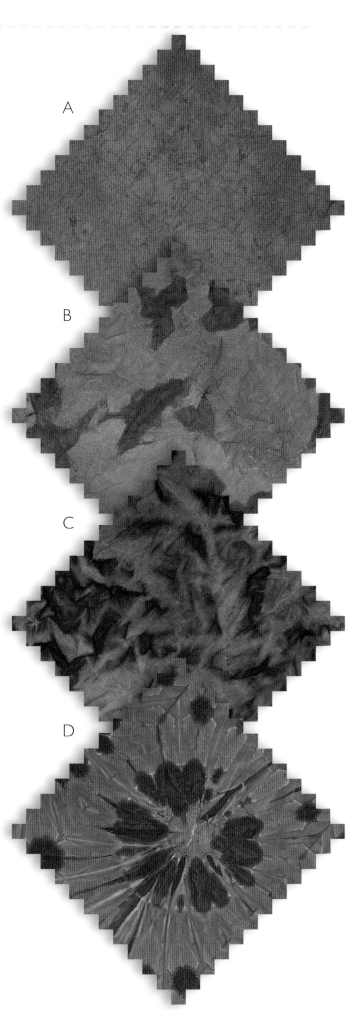

Fuchsia, Red, Brown – Envelope Fold

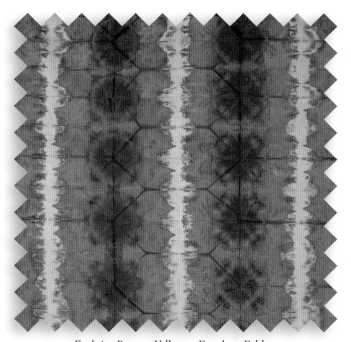

Fuchsia, Brown, Yellow – Envelope Fold

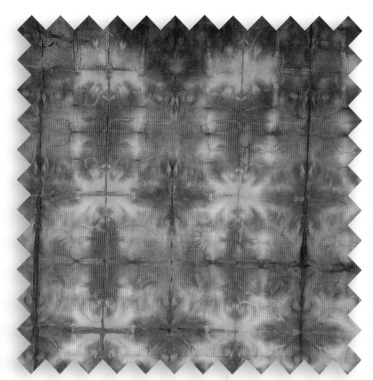

Fuchsia, Aqua – Checkerboard Fold

Fuchsia, Yellow, Blue – Multiple Circle Fold

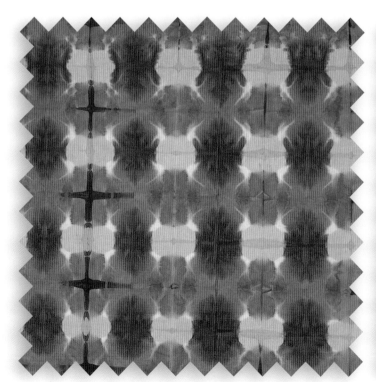

Fuchsia, Red, Yellow, Blue – Checkerboard Fold

Fuchsia, Blue – Fan Fold Variation

Blues

Blue Pure Hue – Solid Hand Dyed

Blue Tint – Solid Hand Dyed

Blue Shade – Solid Hand Dyed

Blue, Green, Red, Yellow – Triangle Fold

Blue, Purple, Golden Yellow, Red – Triangle Fold

Blue, Red – Concentric Circle Fold

Blue Tint, Yellow – Multiple Circle Fold

Blue, Red, Green – Mandala Fold

Blue, Black – Random Line Fold

Blue, Violet – Fan Fold Variation

Blue, Fuchsia, Green, Red – Checkerboard Fold

Oranges

Top to bottom at right:
A – Orange Pure Hue – Solid Hand Dyed
B – Orange Tint – Solid Hand Dyed
C – Orange, Yellow – Random Line Fold
D – Orange, Brown – Fan Fold

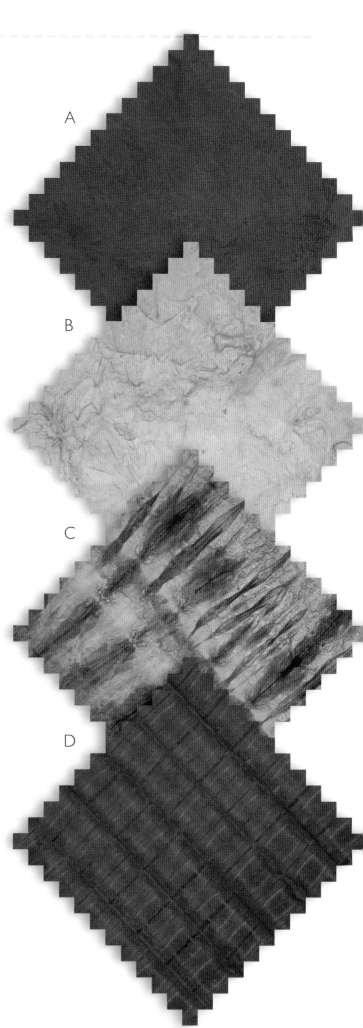

Orange, Green – Concentric Circle Fold

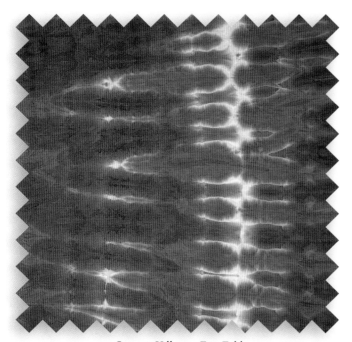

Orange, Yellow – Fan Fold

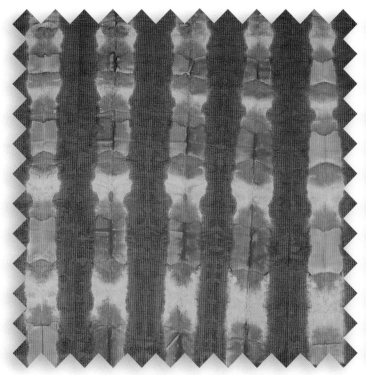

Orange, Green, Blue – Fan Fold

Orange, Blue, Green, Red, Yellow – Random Line Fold

Orange, Yellow, Blue – Triangle Fold

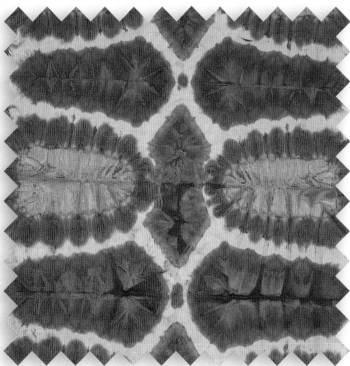

Orange, Green, Yellow, Brown – Multiple Circle Fold

Golden Yellows

Yellow Pure Hue – Solid Hand Dyed   *Yellow Tint – Solid Hand Dyed*   *Yellow Shade – Solid Hand Dyed*

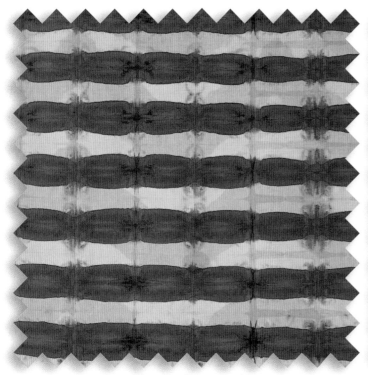

Yellow, Purple – Fan Fold

Yellow, Green, Blue – Mandala Fold

Yellow, Red, Blue – Mandala Fold

Yellow, Red – Random Line Fold

Yellow, Brown – Fan Fold Variation

Yellow, Red, Purple – Fan Fold Variation

Yellow, Caribbean Blue, Brown – Envelope Fold

Greens

Green Pure Hue – Solid Hand Dyed   *Green Tint – Solid Hand Dyed*   *Green, Yellow – Triangle Fold*

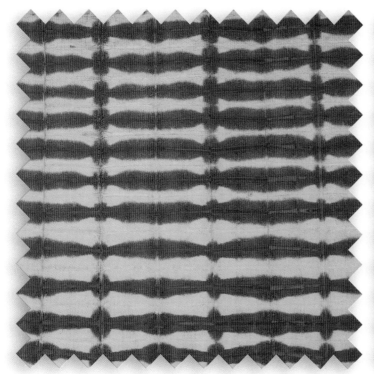

Green, Red – Fan Fold

Green, Blue, Red, Yellow – Random Line Fold

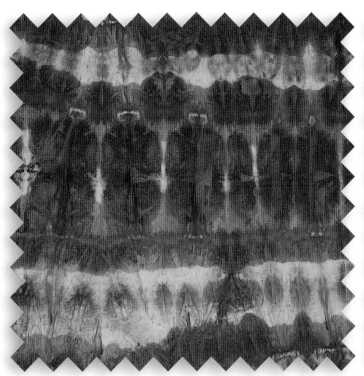

Green, Blue, Red – Random Line Fold

Green, Red, Yellow – Multiple Circle Fold

Green, Blue – Random Line Fold

Green, Dark Blue – Multiple Circle Fold

Purples

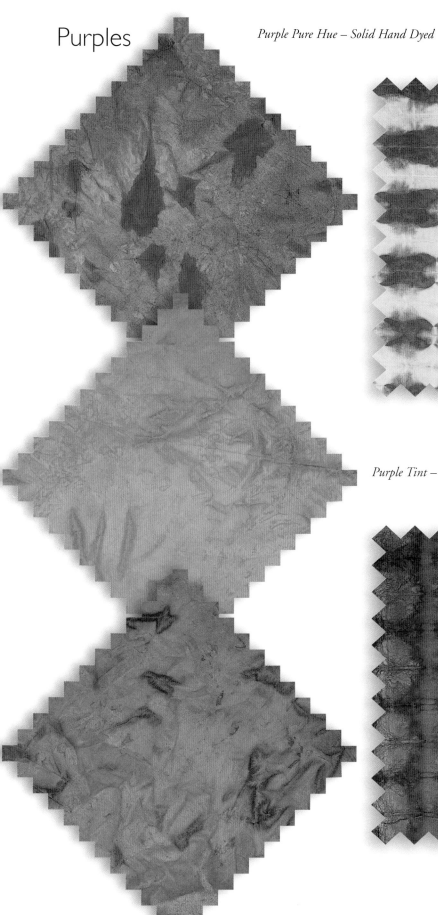

Purple Pure Hue – Solid Hand Dyed

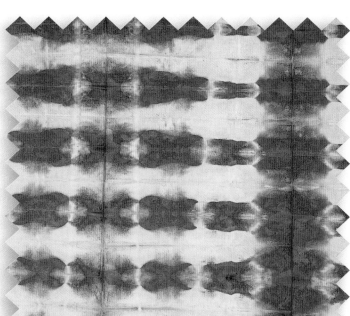

Purple, Blue Tint, Yellow – Fan Fold

Purple Tint – Solid Hand Dyed

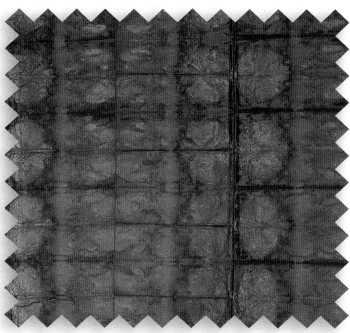

Purple, Red Violet – Fan Fold

Purple Tone – Solid Hand Dyed

Purple, Blue – Fan Fold Variation

Purple, Red, Yellow, Blue Tint – Random Line Fold

Purple, Red, Golden Yellow – Checkerboard Fold

Purple, Brown – Random Line Fold

Purple, Blue, Purple Tint – Checkerboard Fold

Blacks

Black Pure Hue – Solid Hand Dyed   *Black, Red, White – Envelope Fold*   *Black, Blue, Yellow – Fan Fold*

Black, Yellow, Brown – Random Line Fold   *Black, Red, Yellow – Mandala Fold*

Browns

Brown Pure Hue – Solid Hand Dyed　　　　*Brown, Red, Yellow – Triangle Fold*　　　　*Brown, Blue, Orange Tint – Checkerboard Fold*

Brown, Blue, Green – Multiple Circle Fold　　　　*Brown, Yellow, Green – Multiple Circle Fold*

Drip Painting

Drip painting is another way to make ordinary fabric extraordinary.
Air brush paint colors diluted in different concentrations can be
dripped on fabric with great results. Start with 1 ounce of
paint to ½ ounce of water. Use one or two colors.

*Pictured above: FIX Diluted Air Brush Paint, Fabric, Squeeze
Bottle, Disposable Gloves, Newsprint, ½ ounce of Water, Spray
Bottle with Water*

How to:

1. Place the fabric on unprinted newsprint on a protected surface. Tape the corners to secure.

2. Using a spray bottle, spray water lightly over the surface of the fabric. (Photo 1)

3. Hold the squeeze bottle over the fabric and let droplets of the paint solution fall onto the fabric. (Photo 2) Depending upon how damp the fabric is, the drops

Photo 1. Spraying the fabric with water.

will sit there or spread. You can use a hair dryer on high to speed up the drying process.

4. Add a second color. (Photo 3) Allow to dry.

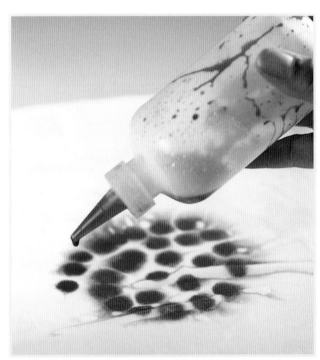

 TIPS:
- Don't throw away that empty spray window cleaner bottle – recycle it!
- You can use a hair dryer on high to quickly dry the fabric. Presto! You are ready to sew.

Photo 2. Dropping paint onto the fabric from the tip of a squirt bottle.

Photo 3. Finished drip-painted fabric.

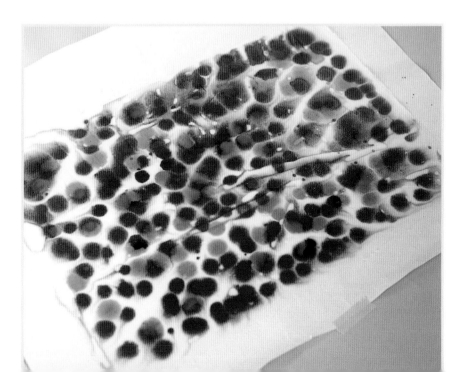

Masking

Masking with freezer paper is another way to create design on fabric. Freezer paper is white paper that has one side coated with a plastic film. You can buy it at the grocery store. When ironed on fabric with the plastic side down, the paper temporarily sticks to the fabric. When you apply the dye, the freezer paper acts as a resist.

You can use a cut piece of freezer paper like a stencil to isolate areas of your fabric from color absorption as you dab paint with a sponge brush. This technique works best with small pieces of fabric (½ yard or less) because they are easier to handle. You can use opaque, metallic, or iridescent air brush paint.

Supplies

Freezer Paper, unprinted newsprint, Fabric, Scissors, undiluted air brush paint, Sponge Brush, Paper Plate, Disposable Gloves, Hair Dryer (Optional).

How to

1. Cut out shapes from the freezer paper.
2. Iron the shapes on the fabric you wish to stencil. Use a dry iron (no steam) on the high setting. (Photo 1)

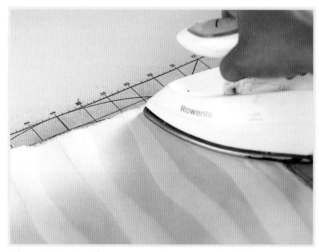

Photo 1. Pressing freezer paper shapes onto the fabric.

3. Place the fabric on unprinted newsprint on a protected surface. Pour a small amount of un-diluted air brush paint on a disposable plate. (Even though I'm not wearing gloves in this photograph, wearing gloves to protect your hands is a good idea.)
4. Load the tip of a sponge brush with paint. Dab paint on the exposed areas of the fabric with an up-and-down motion. (Photo 2) Take care to keep paint from getting under the stencil by painting away from the stencil, not towards it – start with the edge of the sponge on the stencil and pull away. Keep dabbing until you have covered the areas you want painted.

Photo 2. Dabbing paint on the fabric with a foam brush.

5. You can let the stenciled fabric air dry (this takes 10 to 30 minutes), or you can dry it with a hair dryer for 15 to 20 seconds. (Instantly, you'll have an interesting piece of fabric to work with.) Remove the freezer paper when the fabric is dry.

Dyeing Terminology

Acrylic – A substance or surface containing thermoplastic, polymeric compounds, such as paints or textiles.

Airbrush Paint – Pigmented substance containing acrylic compounds, used to air brush, tie dye, paint, print, or stencil.

Dilute – To thin or weaken by the addition of a liquid. (In our case, water.)

Direct Application Process – Method of coloring fabric in which diluted dye or pigment is applied to fabric with a squeeze bottle or by pouring.

Dye – Pigment used to impart a particular color to cloth. Pigments may be obtained from natural substances in plants, animals, and minerals or produced artificially from coal-tar substances.

Fiber Reactive Dyes – Chemically formulated dyes that bond with the fibers of fabric when used with caustic soda.

Hand Dyeing – The process of manipulating and coloring fabric completely by hand, without the use of power-driven machinery.

Heat Setting – Using a, iron with a metal soleplate on the high setting or drying in a commercial dryer for 45 minutes on the hottest setting to make the fabric washable and colorfast.

Immersion Process – The method of coloring fabric in which fabric is submerged in buckets of water with dye added to soak and take up the dye. A caustic chemical, soda ash, is used in the process.

Migrate – To move from one area to another. In dyeing, water is the medium that allows the pigment to migrate through the fabric and between the folds.

Natural Fabrics – Fabrics that originate from plants, animals, or insects, e.g., cotton, linen, rayon, silk, and wool.

Opaque – Condition in which pigment has additives that allow it to cover the fabric no matter what color it is.

Pigment – A substance used for coloring is mixed with a liquid medium to make paint.

Saturated – Containing the maximum amount of liquid a fabric can hold without dripping.

Shibori – Dyeing techniques originating in Japan that involve the manipulation of fabric by folding, tucking, sewing, clamping, and binding.

Solution – Homogenous mixture of two or more substances in a liquid form.

Stencil – A thin sheet of metal or paper in which openings are cut so that when paint is applied, it passes through the openings to create a design.

Textile – Fabric made by weaving, knitting, etc. that has color, design, and/or embellishments.

Tie Dyeing – The technique in which dye, folds, gathers, and bindings are used to create mottled color and design on fabric.

Transparent – Condition of pigmented paint that allows other colors to show through.

Waterbased – Any preparation that contains water as the liquefying agent.

CHAPTER 3

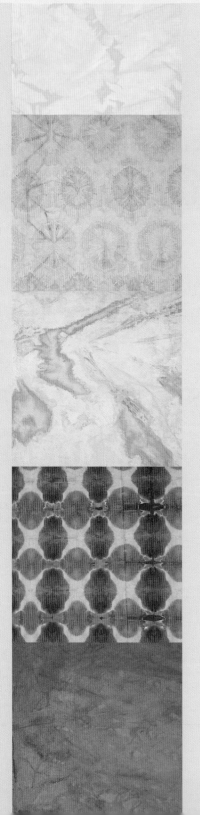

Quilting Basics

A QUILT IS LIKE A SANDWICH. It has three layers: a top, which is made by assembling individual pieced blocks and then joining the blocks to create the top; the filling, called batting, that provides dimension and loft, and the backing, which is usually a minimally pieced (if the quilt is large) or solid (if the quilt is small) expanse of fabric. This chapter shows the basic processes of assembling a top and stitching the layers together.

The world of quilting is vast! As you begin the process of quilting, be aware that there are many ways to perform the tasks involved. The methods I use were passed on to me from my grandmother. I continue to use them, hoping to achieve the look and style of my grandmother's quilts. There is so much to learn and lots of room for growth and development.

New tools become available and techniques evolve constantly. Try them, and see what works best for you.

Quilting Supplies

Scissors

Get a sharp, comfortable pair of **shears** for cutting fabric. A small pair of **embroidery scissors** will also come in handy. TIP: Use a small pair of **nail clippers** to cut threads when traveling.

Rotary Cutting Tools

A **rotary cutting tool** has a razor-edge wheel that is very sharp and should not be used carelessly. Several types are available. Check out the options and choose the type most comfortable for you.

A rotary cutter comes with a guard – make a special effort to close it each time you finish cutting and keep it out of the reach of children. Purchase the largest **cutting mat** your sewing area can accommodate to use with your rotary cutter. Do not roll it up or store it in direct sunlight.

Continued on next page

Quilting Supplies, continued

There are a variety of heavy, plastic **rotary rulers** in different shapes and sizes that you can use with a rotary cutter that help you cut accurate pieces. My favorites are 6" x 24" and 12½" square.

Pattern Making Supplies

You can use **template plastic or cardboard** to create templates for tracing shapes on the fabric prior to cutting.

Use **graph paper** to draw quilting block or quilt designs. Try ¼" graph paper to start. **Colored pencils** allow you to color your designs so that you can see if your color scheme is pleasing to you.

Needles

You need **hand sewing needles** and **machine sewing needles**. Needles come in sizes designated by numbers. For hand sewing needles, the larger the number, the smaller the needle. For sewing machine needles, the opposite is true – the larger the number, the larger the needle.

For sewing machine piecing, use size 75/11 or 80/12 sewing machine needles. For hand piecing, use sharps. I suggest you begin with a size 11 hand sewing needle. For hand quilting, use the needles called "betweens" – they are shorter than sharps. Begin with a size 8 or 9.

Pins

Use **rust-proof safety pins** for pin-basting the three quilt layers together. You will need hundreds for a big quilt. Use 1" or 2" safety pins.

Use **long, thin straight pins** to join fabric and fabric pieces. A **pin cushion** is a good, safe place to stick pins and needles.

Thread

Use **medium-weight sewing thread** for hand and machine piecing. Select an all-cotton or cotton-covered polyester thread in a color that blends with the color(s) of your fabrics. For piecing, you can also use white thread on light fabrics, black thread on dark fabrics, and medium gray or beige for the colors in-between. When using solid fabrics, select thread to match.

The thread used for hand quilting is called **quilting thread** and is stiffer than regular sewing thread. You can choose all-cotton or a polyester-cotton blend. You can also try **embroidery floss**, **pearl cotton**, or some of the new **metallic threads** used for fine needlework for quilting.

Thread for machine quilting can be either **lightweight cotton thread** or a **monofilament nylon thread** used both in the needle and in the bobbin. Monofilament nylon thread comes in clear for light-colored projects and smoke for dark-colored projects.

Fabric Marking Instruments

There are many types of marking instruments available – try some out to see what works best for you. Before marking the top of your quilt with any marking tool, always test it on a scrap of the fabric you are quilting to make sure can easily remove the marks.

I often use **tailor's chalk**. Sometimes when I'm working with lines, I'll use a ruler and mark by scratching the line I want to quilt with a safety pin. The line guides my quilting but goes away after a while.

Other Sewing Tools

Use a **thimble** to protect your finger when you are hand sewing. One size does not fit all fingers – choose a style and size that's comfortable to you.

A **seam ripper** makes it easy to remove a line of stitching if and when you make a mistake.

Batting

Batting is the soft layer between the front and back of the quilt. It can be made of cotton, polyester, poly-cotton blends, silk, or wool. It comes in low loft (thin) and high loft (thick).

Ironing Tools

You'll need an **iron** and a **pressing surface**. Choose an iron that can be adjusted to a cotton setting and used with or without steam. Use a firm surface for ironing pieced fabrics and a soft surface, like a towel, to iron appliquéd fabric.

Basic Techniques

Cutting the Fabric

I approach cutting two ways. I either use the pattern of the fabric as a design element and strategically cut well-positioned fabric pieces or I cut with abandon and am surprised at the outcome. Try both ways and see which works for you. Many times, quilters tell me they are hesitant to cut tie-dyed fabrics. Don't be. If you are using a pattern, follow its cutting directions for maximum accuracy.

Use a rotary cutter or shears to cut your fabrics for piecing. Here are some helpful things to know:

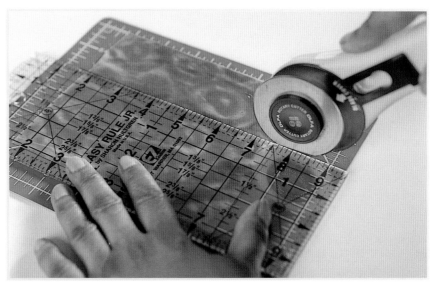

Cutting fabric with rotary cutter.

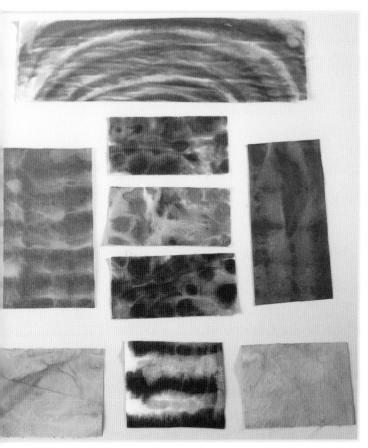

The pieces for a block laid out as they will be joined.

Find the Fabric Grain

Locating the straight-of-grain helps you line up rulers for cutting and position templates.

The **lengthwise grain** runs parallel to the selvedges and has very little stretch. The **crosswise grain** runs perpendicular to the selvedges and has a slight amount of stretch. Both the lengthwise grain and the crosswise grain are considered straight-of-grain. You need the straight-of-grain on your patchwork pieces to go vertically or horizontally. The **diagonal grain** runs at a 45-degree angle to the straight-of-grain and is called the true bias. True bias stretches. Diagonally cut fabrics are stretchy and must be handled with care.

There Is No Right Side

A special quality of hand-dyed fabric is that both the front and back of the fabric are beautiful with very little variation. Sometimes one side is a little lighter than the other. This could be to the quilter's advantage – you could get a color plus its lighter counterpart from the same piece of fabric.

Piecing the Fabric

You can sew together the pieces for your quilt by machine or by hand. Follow the instructions for piecing given with the pattern, picking up the pieces as needed and sewing

Continued on next page

Piecing the Fabric, continued

them together. To make piecing easier and avoid confusion, lay out the pieces on your work table as they will appear when the block or section is completed. As you work, put the pieces you have sewn together back in the layout with the other un-sewn pieces until the pattern is complete.

When you have completed piecing the blocks, sew the blocks together to assemble the top of the quilt. When making quarter square and half square triangle blocks, the ends of seam allowances will extend past the edges of the block. Trim the ends of the seam allowances even with the edges of the block, then sew the blocks together.

Machine Piecing:

Use a needle suitable for woven fabrics (size 75/11 or 80/12) and make sure the needle is sharp. The standard seam allowance for piecing is ¼". On many sewing machines, there is a mark on the sewing machine face plate to use as a guide to sew ¼" seams. If not, measure ¼" from the needle and mark the spot with a piece of masking tape. This is important because this helps you achieve accuracy. Use regular sewing thread (not quilting thread) for machine piecing.

To begin piecing, place two pieces right sides together and match the raw edges. Pin the pieces together and sew from one edge to the other edge, removing the straight pins as you get close to them. Do not sew over pins! Doing so could break the needle or damage the face plate of your sewing machine. TIP: If you are strip piecing, as you sew each strip to the strip set, alternate the end at which you begin sewing. This helps to control the curving distortion common in strip piecing.

Hand Piecing:

For accuracy, mark the seam allowance ¼" from the edge of the fabric pieces. To begin, thread a single length of thread into a hand sewing needle and make a small knot at one end. Place two pieces right sides together and carefully match the drawn lines. Pin the pieces together. Take a backstitch at one end of the drawn line. Using a running stitch (7 to 10 stitches per inch), stitch the pieces together along the line. With practice, your stitches will become straight and even. Backstitch at the end of the line of stitching. Knot and cut your thread.

Pressing

Proper pressing can lead to easier hand quilting with less bulk. Here are some guidelines to help you decide how and when to press your seam allowances:

• When machine piecing, press seam allowances as you sew. When hand piecing, press after you have completed a section or a block.

• Generally, it's best to press your seam allowances to one side to make your seams strong, and to press toward the darker fabric. To reduce bulk, sometimes you must press the seam open or to the lighter side. If so, trim the darker edges a little lower than the lighter edge so that it won't show through on the right side when quilted.

• When you are matching seams to sew rows together, seam allowances face in the same direction when sewing rows. After sewing, the fabric is opened out and layed flat, pressing the allowances all in one direction.

Pressing a seam to one side.

Assembling the Quilt Sandwich

Once you have finished piecing your quilt top, it is time to assemble and baste the layers together for quilting. It's a good idea to let your batting breathe by taking it out of the bag an hour or more before you want to use it. This prevents deep creases in the quilt later on.

Basting holds the layers together while you stitch the quilt. There are several ways to baste – with a needle and thread, with safety pins, or with a spray adhesive product you can buy in quilting stores. Do not needle-and-thread baste or safety pin baste on your best wooden table top! The pins and needles could damage the wood.

If you're going to use a needle and thread or safety pins, to baste, begin your quilt sandwich by laying the backing fabric on a large table, wrong side up. Tape the backing fabric in place with masking tape at the ends and at intervals along the sides. Place the piece of batting on top of the backing. Smooth it by rubbing from the center out, feeling for wrinkles. Lay the quilt top on the batting. Adjust the batting, quilt top and backing, making sure to smooth all three layers from the center out.

Needle-and-Thread Basting. Thread a needle with thread in a contrasting color and tie a good knot in it. Sew diagonally across the sandwich using really big running stitches. Also, sew from side to side three times, with space between the rows of stitches. Then sew really big running stitches all around the edges of your quilt sandwich. This will hold the layers in place while you stitch with a hoop or on a quilting frame.

Safety Pin Basting. With this method, you take dozens of 1" or 2" safety pins and pin them through all the layers of the quilt, spacing them two inches apart. Start at one end of your quilt sandwich and work across it, smoothing the layers as you pin. Keep pinning until you get to the other side. When you're finished, you can stitch with a hoop, on a frame, or neither for an "already used" look.

Spray Adhesive Basting. This method works best for small projects. Enlist the help of a friend and work in an area with good ventilation! Start by taping down the backing as described previously. Spray the wrong side of the backing with the quilting adhesive, then lay your batting in place. Spray the surface of the batting, and lay your quilt top over it. Smooth it out, making sure there are no wrinkles. (You may reposition the top, if needed.) Pull the tape ends away from the edge of the backing and you are ready to quilt.

A quilt sandwich.

A quilt that has been safety-pin basted.

Quilting by Hand

Hand quilting results in noticeable stitches and a soft look. There are many methods of hand quilting so adapt the techniques I describe to suit your needs. The more you hand quilt, the easier it becomes. If you are new to the process, develop your quilting style with straight lines or echo the design of the quilt top. Small, evenly spaced stitches fit some quilters' aesthetics, while other quilters make larger stitches as a design element in their quilts. A beginner should strive for evenly spaced, uniform-size stitches. As you gain experience, your quilting stitches will generally decrease in size. Don't worry about the size of your stitches. Remember, enjoy your quilting!

Some hand quilters hold their basted quilts loosely in their hands as they sew. This method is called "lap quilting." Others use wooden hoops or frames to hold the basted quilt layers together, keeping them smooth and evenly firm. Hand quilters most often use a size 10 or 12 "in-between" needle and 100% cotton hand quilting or sewing thread. Stitch with an 18" length of thread in your needle.

Here's how:

1. Begin your stitches by backstitching and burying the thread tail between the layers of the quilt on the back side. Wear a thimble for ease of quilting. Pull the needle through the layers to the front of the quilt.
2. Sew, using the running stitch and following your chosen design. Remember that uniformity is more important than the actual length of the stitches.
3. When you are near the end of the thread, sew through the layers until you come out the back of the quilt. Make three backstitches in the same place. Sew through the layers, burying the tail of your thread, and come out of the quilt. Trim the thread close to the quilt back.

Variations

Seed Beads: Sew seed beads as you quilt by sewing a few stitches, picking up a bead on your needle and sewing it to your quilt with three stitches. Continue quilting, repeating this as you desire.

Other Threads: You can also use embroidery floss or pearl cotton thread for hand quilting. If you do, use an embroidery needle, sizes 7 to 10.

Tying Off: Instead of sewing rows of stitches, you can tie off your quilt, making a pattern of knots with pearl cotton or floss. Try using size 14 to 15 long darner needles.

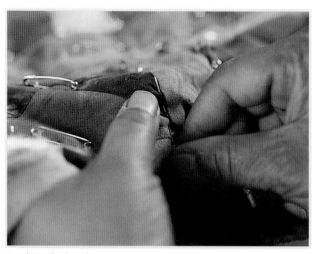

Quilting by hand.

Binding the Edges

After all the quilting is done, it is time to bind the raw edges of the quilt. There are many ways to bind, some more complex than others. Here, I share two ways that my grandmother taught me.

Fold Over Self Binding

For this easy binding technique, cut your backing at least 2" larger on all sides than the quilt top. When you sandwich your layers for quilting, center the top and batting on the backing fabric.

1. When you have finished quilting, sew all around the edge of the quilt to stabilize it.
2. Trim the batting to the edge of the quilt top. (Photo 1)

Photo 1. Trimming the batting.

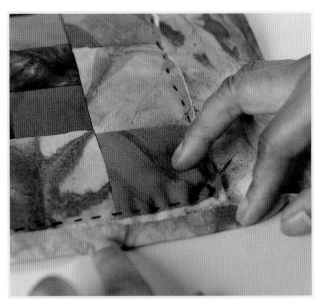

Photo 2. Folding and finger pressing the backing fabric up to the raw edge.

Photo 3. Blind stitching the binding.

3. Trim the backing so it is 1" wide on all four sides.
4. Turn ½" forward (towards the quilt) on all four sides and finger press. (Photo 2)
5. Fold again, bringing the backing fabric over the raw quilt edge of the quilt. Safety pin it every 2".
6. Use a blind stitch to sew the binding to the quilt top on all sides. (Photo 3)
7. When you reach the end, sew through to the back. At the point where the needle and thread come out the back, do three back stitches, and run your needle between the layers to bury the tail in the batting. Come out the back and clip your thread. ❏

Straight Grain Binding

This binding uses a separate strip of fabric to cover the edges of the quilt sandwich. You can make the binding from the same fabric you used for the backing or from any fabric – hand-dyed, patterned, or solid – of your choice.

1. When you have finished quilting, sew all around the edge of the quilt to stabilize it.
2. To find out how much binding is required, measure the perimeter of your quilt and add 10".
3. Cut strips 2" wide across the width of your binding fabric. Cut the ends of the strips at a 45-degree angle. Sew the strips together, making one long strip that is the perimeter measure plus the additional 10".
4. Press open the seams and trim off the points at the ends of the seams.
5. Fold the strip in half lengthwise, with wrong sides together, and press.
6. Place the binding on the front of the quilt starting at the middle of the bottom edge. Align the raw edges of the binding with the raw edges of the quilt. Machine sew the binding to the quilt with a ¼" seam allowance (Photo 1), leaving the first 3" of the binding loose so you can join the beginning and ending of the binding strip when you finish.

continued on next page

Photo 1. Machine sewing the binding strip to the front of the quilt with the right sides together.

Photo 2. Mitering a corner.

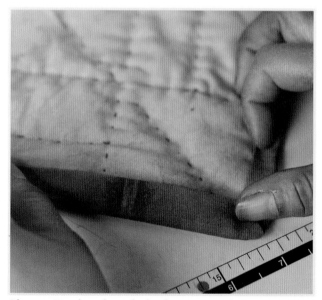

Photo 3. Hand stitching the binding strip on the back of the quilt.

Hanging a Quilt

To prevent fading or fabric deterioration, do not hang your quilt in direct sunlight, in constant, bright artificial light, or in very humid spaces. Vacuum it occasionally to prevent dust buildup.

Straight Grain Binding, continued

7. When you are ¼" from the corner of the quilt, stop stitching and backstitch. Turn the quilt to sew the next edge. Fold the binding with all the raw edges even on the next side. (Photo 2) This will make a fold in the corner with one side at 45 degrees. Continue sewing, repeating the folding at each corner.

8. As you come around and meet the beginning of the binding, stop, remove the needle, clip the thread, and join the bindings. To do this, open the folds, putting right sides together where they meet. Estimate where you need to sew to make the binding fit. Sew and cut off the excess. Press the seam allowance open. Return the seamed strip to the edge of the quilt and finish sewing the binding to the quilt top.

9. Fold the binding to the back of the quilt, covering the raw edges and your stabilizing stitches.

10. Using thread that matches the color of the binding, thread a hand sewing needle with a single strand of sewing thread about 18" long. Knot one end. Blind stitch the binding in place so only tiny stitches are visible on the binding. (Photo 3) ❏

Making a Sleeve for Hanging

If you want to display your quilt as a wall hanging, the weight of the quilt must be balanced. To do this, attach a fabric sleeve to the back of the quilt after the quilt is finished. The sleeve can hold a dowel or decorative rod for hanging. Here's how:

Choose a fabric that's one of the colors in the quilt. Cut a strip 12" deep and as long as the width of the quilt. Turn under and stitch ½" double-fold hems at each short end. (Making a sleeve that's a little less wide than the quilt means the rod will be invisible and not extend beyond the sides of the quilt.) Stitch the long edges, wrong sides together, with a ½" seam. Press the seam allowance open. Turn the sleeve so that the long seam allowance is at the center back of the sleeve (and against the back of the quilt when sewn on). Press it flat.

Locate the middle of the sleeve and the middle of the quilt. Line up the sleeve ½" from the top of the quilt, with its middle touching the middle of the quilt. Pin in place. Sew the sleeve to the back of the quilt along both long edges, using an overcast stitch or a ladder stitch. Stitch

through the backing, into the batting, being careful not to sew through to the front of the quilt. Don't sew the edges of the sleeve shut. Reinforce the top and bottom ends with extra stitches for added strength.

CHAPTER 4

Artistic Embellishments

YOU HAVE HAND-DYED some unique fabric, pieced an awe-inspiring quilt top, and made a beautiful little quilt. Now you can take it to the next level with artistic embellishments. I call this "adding another layer of love."

Embellishments give greater dimension to quilts. This chapter shows some of my favorite embellishment techniques.

Yo-Yos

Yo-yos are circular, three-dimensional elements that can be sewn together to create blocks or panels or appliqued as desired to your quilts. You can cut circles of one size or various sizes to try out the technique.

Supplies

- Fabric circles, 6" diameter
- 100% cotton sewing thread *or* embroidery floss
- Scissors
- *Optional:* Beads or a button

How to

1. Thread a needle with a length of thread twice the circumference of the fabric circle. Tie a knot at the end of the thread. With the wrong side of the fabric facing you, sew medium-size running stitches all around the circle of fabric about ¼" from the edge. (Photo 1) **Note:** I do not hem the edges of the fabric circle before gathering because I want the center to have less bulk and lay flat to accommodate buttons or beads.

2. When you've completed the circle, pull the thread to draw up the stitches. (Photo 2) Flatten and fluff up the yo-yo, then stitch in the middle, catching the folds as you go around about eight times.

3. Sew into the center through to the back with a backstitch three times. (Photo 3)

4. *Optional:* Add beads or a button. Come back up through the center. Sew a button in the center, stitching through it several times to secure it, or sew on beads one at a time with three stitches in each bead. Finish off by coming back through to the back, sewing three backstitches, and clipping the thread to complete the process. ❏

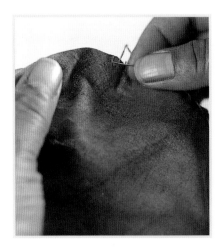

Photo 1. Sewing a running stitch around edge of fabric circle. **Note:** *For demonstration purposes, I used a lighter colored thread instead of matching thread so the stitches would be easier to see.*

Photo 2. Pulling the thread to gather the circle.

Photo 3. Sewing the center.

Beading

Beads can make an ordinary quilt exciting. They are easy to find, and since they don't have a shelf life they are great to collect. I use glass beads, really nice plastic beads, and semi-precious gemstone beads. I stay away from natural seed and wooden beads because bugs might like eating them or they may be acidic. Beads can fade, too. Check them for colorfastness by placing a few of them in a warm, wet white paper towel for a while to see if color comes off on the paper towel.

You can get beads at craft stores or bead shops; however, recycling old jewelry is a great place to find something unusual. Select lightweight beads that will not make your quilt sag. There are many styles and types of beads – the sky is the limit!

Do not put beads on quilts made for babies and young children – they can be a choking hazard!

Supplies
- Finished quilt
- 100% cotton all purpose thread
- Marking pencil
- Sharp needle, size 10
- Seed beads, 5mm
- Pencil *or* chalk *or* fabric marker

How to
1. Decide where you want the beads to be and make dots to mark the places. Thread your needle with a double strand of thread.
2. Go into the back of the quilt with the threaded needle ½" from where you want to come out. Draw out your needle, leaving the tails of your doubled thread hanging until you have secured your knot. Then backstitch three times at the place where you came out. Go through the layers to the top at the desired location and pull the thread snug.
3. Place a bead on the needle and slide it to the surface of the quilt. Then go back in the same area and go through the bead again for a total of three times. Stitch through to the back of the quilt and make a small stitch to secure the bead.
4. Travel with the needle between the backing and the batting one needle-length away from the first bead. Come out on the top and repeat the process again until the area is beaded to your satisfaction.
5. When you have three or four inches of thread left on the needle, stop that series of beads so that you can reload your needle with a new length of thread. Sew through to the back. Backstitch three times in the spot where the thread is coming out. Let your needle travel between the backing and the batting to bury the tail, come out of the back, and clip the thread. ❑

Sewing More than One Bead at a Time
If you decide to sew on more than one bead at a time, more than five in a group may be problematic. After the first long stitch through all the beads, go back and sew through each bead individually. Then sew through them all at least two more times. This is not being excessive – this is securing your embellishments for the life of the quilt.

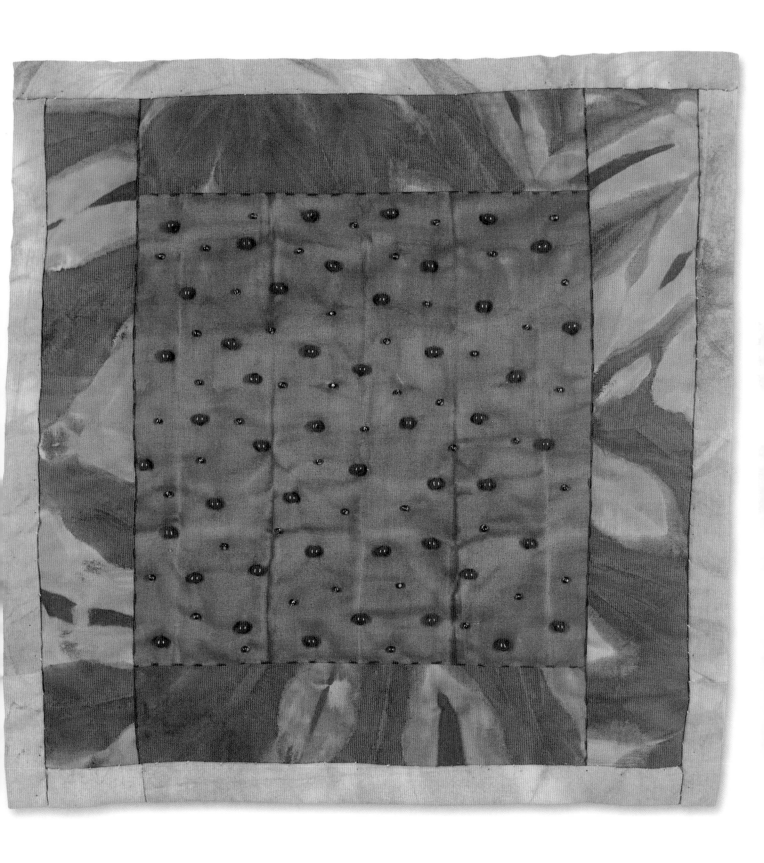

Interfacing Applique

Interfacing applique is great when you are creating large shapes with fairly smooth edges and pieces with curves – you'll have neatly finished edges and a sturdy shape. You can attach the appliques by hand or with a sewing machine. The squares on this sampler are attached with this technique.

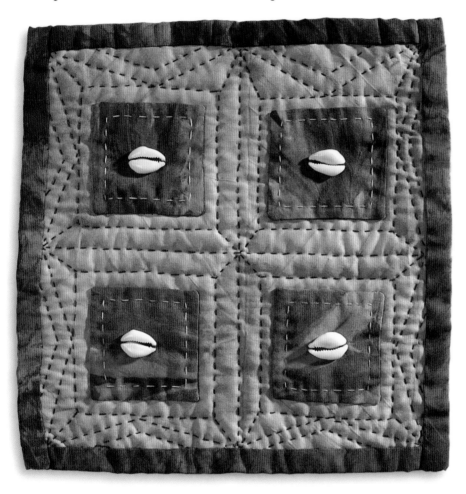

Supplies

- Lightweight non-woven interfacing (NOT fusible)
- Fabrics for applique and background
- Scissors
- Long, thin straight pins
- Needle *or* sewing machine
- Sewing thread
- Pencil

How to

1. Trace the applique shape on lightweight interfacing. Cut out the shape about ½" outside of the drawn line.
2. Position the interfacing on the right side of the fabric. Stitch along the drawn line through both layers.
3. Trim excess fabric, leaving a ¼" seam allowance. Clip the curves so the piece will lie flat.
4. Cut a slit in the center of the interfacing. Turn the shape right side out through the slit. Press the shape flat.
5. Position the applique on the background. Pin and sew in place, using a blind stitch or small machine stitch. ❑

Four Stages of Interfacing Applique
Pictured left to right, top row:
Fabric and interfacing
Design sewn onto layers of fabric and interfacing.

Pictured left to right, bottom row:
Excess fabric and interfacing trimmed from sewn design.
Applique turned right side out.

Curved Pieces
On curved pieces, clip the curves so the piece will lie flat when it is turned right side out and ironed.

Paper Bag Applique

Here's a way to recycle thick brown paper bags. Use them to create circular paper shapes to gather fabric circles around. This technique simplifies sewing circular applique shapes on a quilt because the paper gives some rigidity to the fabric circle, making it easier to handle.

Supplies

▨ Brown Paper Bag
▨ Fabric circles
▨ Fabric scissors
▨ Paper scissors
▨ 100% cotton thread
▨ Hand sewing needle
▨ Long straight pins

How to

1. Using paper scissors (not your good fabric scissors), cut out a 2" diameter brown paper circle. Using fabric scissors, cut a 2½" diameter fabric circle.

2. Thread a needle with a single strand of thread; tie a knot at the end. Using a running stitch, sew around the edge of the fabric circle.

3. Center the paper circle on the fabric circle (Photo 1) and gently pull the thread to draw the thread up snug around the circular paper form. (Photo 2) Do two back-stitches into the fabric circle and clip the thread.

4. Position the circular applique – with the paper circle still in place –

Continued on next page

Photo 1. The paper bag circle on the fabric circle.

Photo 2. The fabric circle gathered around the paper circle.

Photo 3. Sewing the circle applique shape in place.

Paper Bag Appliques, continued

on the fabric. Using a needle threaded with a single strand of thread and knotted at the end, begin by sewing through the back of the circle at the edge. Using very tiny stitches, sew around the circle (Photo 3) until you are about three-quarters of the way around. Be careful not to sew through the paper.

5. At this point, stop, reach under the circle with your needle, and pull out the paper circle. (Photo 4)

6. Continue to sew until you finish attaching the applique. Sew through to the back of the fabric. Backstitch under the circle three times, bring out your needle, and clip the end of the thread. ❑

Photo 4. Using a needle to help pull out the paper bag shape from applique.
Pictured opposite: Appliqued Circles Quilt created using this applique method. See page 120 for project instructions.

Quilting Terminology

Applique – The process of sewing small pieces of fabric on a larger piece of fabric by hand or machine.

Backstitch – Hand stitching back over three or more stitches.

Basting, Safety Pin – Joining the layers of a quilt with safety pins.

Basting, Thread – Joining layers of fabric or the layers of a quilt with long hand stitches before quilting to keep the layers from shifting.

Batting – The filler between two pieces of fabric that forms a quilt and provides warmth. Batting can be cotton, polyester, a poly-cotton blend, silk, or wool.

Bias – The diagonal grain of a woven fabric. True bias is at a 45 degree angle to the selvedges.

Binding – The technique of finishing the edges of the quilt.

Block – The design unit of a quilt top.

Border – A strip of fabric – pieced or not – sewn to the edges of a quilt top to frame it.

Hand Piecing – The process of sewing pieces of fabric together by hand to create quilt blocks or quilt tops.

Machine Piecing – The process of using a sewing machine to sew together pieces of fabric to create quilt blocks or quilt tops.

Quilting – Making small running stitches to hold the layers of a quilt together.

Quilt-in-the-Ditch – Quilting where the seams come together on a quilt.

Quilt Sandwich – The quilt top, batting, and quilt backing, stacked one upon another, in preparation for basting.

Rotary Cutter – A fabric cutting tool with a razor sharp circular blade that can cut through layers of fabric. It must be used with a plastic ruler and mat.

Sashing – The fabric that separates the blocks within a quilt top.

Seam Allowance – The area of fabric between the seam and the raw edge.

Selvedge – The lengthwise finished edge on each side of the fabric.

Sleeve – A fabric tube sewn on the back of a quilt or wallhanging so that it can be hung with a dowel or rod.

Straight of Grain – The lengthwise and crosswise threads of a woven fabric.

Template – A firm pattern piece used as a guide for marking and transferring applique shapes onto fabric.

Yo-Yo – A fabric circle gathered and flattened to form a rosette.

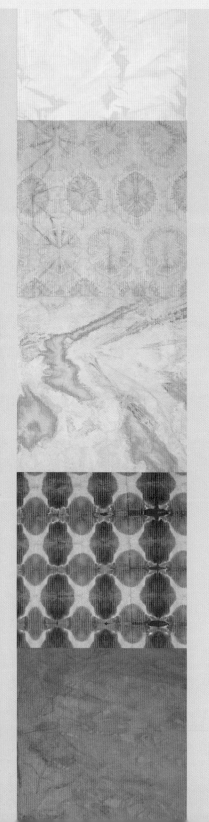

CHAPTER 5

Projects You Can Make

NOW YOU ARE READY to grab your quilting supplies and have some fun. You'll find instructions for a variety of quilting projects, both large and small – a bookmark, an eye glass case, tabletop accessories, pillows, wallhangings. Make them as I did, or use them as a jumping off point for your own unique creations.

The quilts I make all begin with the hand-dyed fabrics. The colors and visual texture that happens in surface-designed fabric inspire me and allow my imagination to flow freely. I'm captivated by flowers and geometric patterns, and I use them as basic design elements to develop original, improvisational quilts and collectibles. I love large designs, asymmetry, and bright colors. I also appreciate and use symbolic forms to share universal wisdom and truth. I understand that art is powerful and it is my hope that my quilts to promote positive thinking, joyful attitudes, and self-transformation. I feel personal satisfaction as I use methods of self-expression that add creative energy to the world without harming its water resources.

Making Bed-Sized Quilts: Many of the quilts I make are for display purposes and they are smaller than bed size. You can make bed-sized quilts from any of my smaller quilts by simply adding additional blocks to make the quilt large enough for your size bed.

A Note about Fabric for the Backing

If you wish you can use hand-dyed pieces for the backing; or you can purchase compatible solid fabrics. For larger quilt projects that need quilt size backing, purchase a white sheet and hand dye or use a coordinating colored sheet.

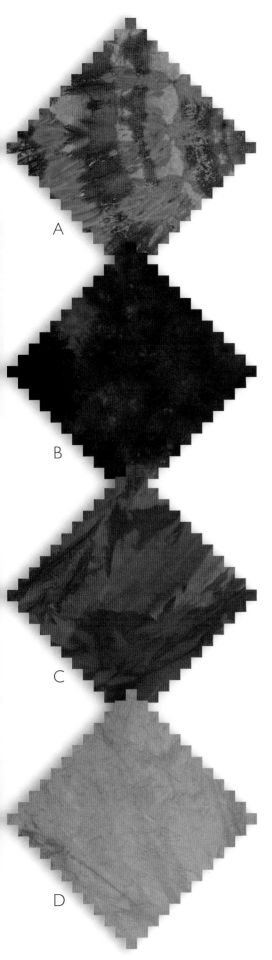

X Marks the Spot Hot Pads

Use these quilted pads to protect your dinner table from hot serving dishes. They were created with four hand-dyed fabrics. The blocks are 7" square.

Swatches of dyed fabric used to make this project, pictured top to bottom:
A – Multi-colored spiral fold tie dyed
B – Dark blue solid hand dyed
C – Red solid hand dyed
D – Green solid hand dyed

Instructions begin on page 70.

X Marks the Spot Hot Pads

Pictured on page 68

Components

For each hot pad:

- Pieced block, 7" square
- Batting, 7½" square
- Backing fabric, 9" square
- 100% cotton thread in a matching color

Cutting the Fabric

1. From the multi-color tie-dyed fabric (A), cut:
   1 square, 4".
   2 strips, each 5" x 2".
2. From the dark blue solid fabric (B), cut:
   2 strips, 5" x 2".
3. From the red solid fabric (C), cut:
   2 strips, each 5" x 2".
4. From the green solid fabric (D), cut:
   2 strips, each 5" x 2",

Piecing the Block

1. Sew the long edges of one fabric strip of each color, plus an additional blue strip (A,B,C,D,B) together to make a five-square piece. See Fig. 1.
2. Sew the long edges of the remaining three fabric strips (A,C,D) together to create a three-color piece.
3. Using a rotary cutter, ruler, and cutting mat, cut the piece in half across seams of the four-color and three-color pieces. See Fig. 1.
4. Sew a three-color strip to each side of the 4" square. Trim excess and press.
5. To complete the block, sew a five-color strip to the top and bottom. Trim away the excess fabric and press.

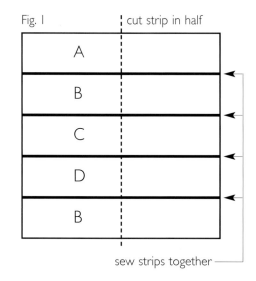

Fig. 1   cut strip in half

sew strips together

Pieces needed for block

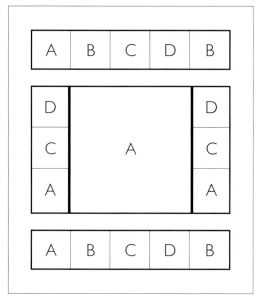

Finished Block

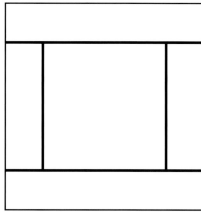

Constructing the Project

1. Make a quilt sandwich with the pieced block, batting, and backing. Make sure the block is centered on the backing. Pin or needle baste.
2. Beginning on one side, sew all around the edge of the block to stabilize it.
3. Quilt-in-the-ditch along all the seams.
4. Trim away the excess batting so the batting piece is the same size as the pieced block.
5. Trim the backing to 1" all around the block.
6. Fold in ½" of the backing fabric on all sides and finger press. Fold the backing ½" over the raw edges of the block. Pin in place.
7. Sew the binding in place with a blind stitch. ❑

Tiny Squares Eye Glass Case

Instructions begin on page 72.

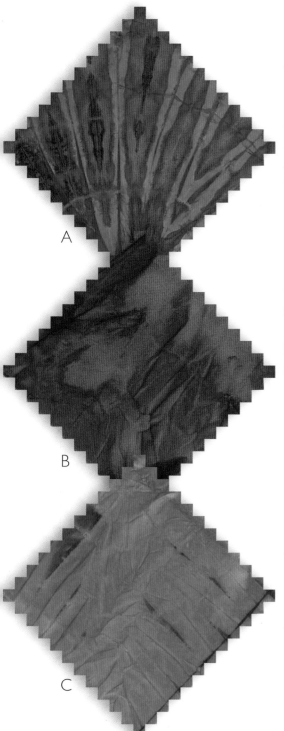

A

B

C

Tiny Squares Eye Glass Case

Wear this case around your neck and use it to hold your reading glasses or sunglasses – no pocket required!

Pictured on page 71

Swatches of dyed fabric used to make this project, pictured top to bottom:
A – Blue and red-violet random line fold tie-dyed
B – Red-violet solid hand-dyed
C – Blue fan fold tie-dyed

Components

- Pieced block, 4¾" x 7½"
- Inside backing fabric, 4¾" x 7½"
- Batting (use an extra piece of fabric), 5" x 8"
- Pocket fabric, 8" x 9"
- 30" braided cord, ⅛" diameter

Optional: Decorative beads

Cutting the Fabric

1. From the blue and red-violet tie-dyed fabric (A), cut:
   1 strip, 1¾" x 4¾".
   3 strips, 1½" x 7½".

2. From the red-violet solid fabric (B), cut:
   3 strips, each 1½" x 7½".

3. From the blue solid fabric (C), cut:
   1 strip, 1½" x 4¾".

Piecing the Block

1. Sew the long sides of the 1½" x 7½" blue and red-violet strips (A) and the red-violet strips (B) together to make a 6-strip set. Press. See Fig. 1.

2. Cut the strip set across the seams into 1½" sections. See Fig. 1. Lay them out as shown in the "Pieces Needed" diagram, adjusting the placement so the seams don't line up. Sew them together to make a block and press.

3. Make a two-strip section with the 1½" x 4¾" blue bar (C) and the 1¾" x 4¾" blue and red-violet tie-dyed bar (A). Sew this to the top of the pieced squares. Press.

4. With wrong sides together, sew the pieced block to the inside backing fabric at the top seam only. Turn right sides out and press.

Constructing the Project

1. Tuck the batting fabric between the pieced block and the inside backing piece.

2. Quilt-in-the-ditch on all seams. Tack the cord at the top on each side of the quilted block.

3. Fold down the top of the pocket fabric ½" and finger press. Fold over another ½" and finger press. Sew this top hem with running stitches.

4. Fold in ½" on the remaining three sides of the pocket fabric and finger press.

5. Lay the quilted block in the center of the pocket fabric. Fold the sides and bottom of the pocket fabric over the raw edges of the block. Finger press and pin in place.

6. Sew the folded edges in place with blind stitches.

7. *Option:* Add beads, as desired. See "Beading" in the "Artistic Embellishments" chapter for instructions on sewing beads. ❑

Fig. 1 – Making the Strip Sets

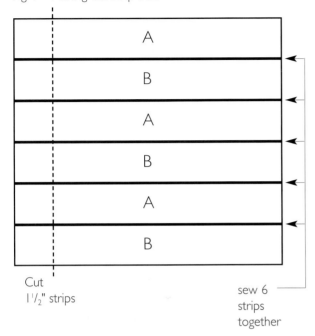

Cut
1½" strips

sew 6
strips
together

Pieces needed

Finished Block

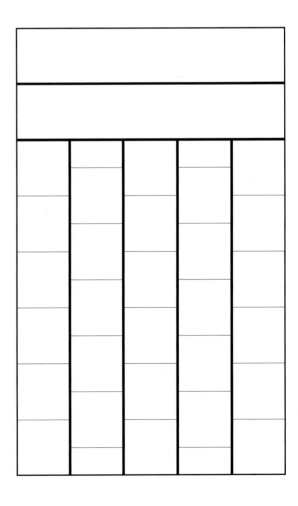

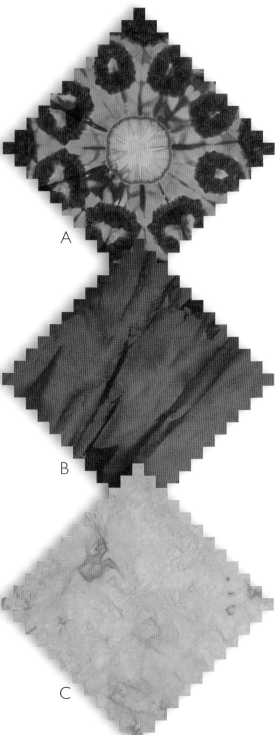

A

B

C

Embellished Bars Pin Cushion

A cowry shell and red seed beads embellish a tiny pillow you can use as a pin cushion.

Swatches of dyed fabric used to make this project, pictured top to bottom:
A – Red, yellow, blue mandala fold tie dyed
B – Red solid hand dyed
C – Leaf green solid hand dyed (1 part yellow, 3 parts green)

Components
- Pieced block, 5½" x 6½"
- Backing fabric, 5½" x 6½"
- Stuffing, about two hands full
- 100% cotton thread in a matching color
- Red seed beads, 4mm
- 1 cowry shell

Cutting the Fabric
1. From the red, yellow, and blue tie dyed (A), cut:
   Three strips, each 1¾" x 4¾".
   Two strips, each 1" x 4".
   Two 2" squares.

2. From the red solid (B), cut:
   Two strips, each 2" x 4¾".
   Two 2" squares.

3. From the leaf green solid (C), cut:
   Two strips, each 1" x 4".
   Two 1½" squares.

Piecing the Block
Make the Shadow Blocks:
These are the blocks in the four corners.
1. On the lighter of the two colors of the 2" squares, draw a diagonal line on the wrong side of each one, corner to corner.
2. Take the other two 2" squares and place one over each square with the drawn line, right sides together. Sew ¼" from the line on each side, backstitching as you begin and end. (Fig. 1) Cut on the line and press. You now have two half-square triangle blocks. (See Fig. 2)
3. On each 1½" leaf green square, draw a diagonal line on the wrong side.
4. Place one leaf green square on each half-square triangle block, with diagonal seam perpendicular to the drawn line on the green square. Sew ¼" from the line on both sides, backstitching as you begin and end. Cut on the line and press. (Fig. 3)

Continued on next page

Embellished Bars Pin Cushion, continued

You now have four 1" pieced shadow blocks. Set them aside.

Sew the Strip Sets:

1. Sew two strip sets composed of one 1" x 4" strip of tie-dyed fabric and one 1" x 4" strip of leaf green. Press.
2. On each end of each strip set, sew a shadow block. Press and trim, if necessary. Set them aside.
3. Create the center strip set by sewing the 4¾" strips together in this order: one tie-dyed strip, one red strip, one tie-dyed strip, one red strip, one tie-dyed strip. Press.
4. Sew a two-strip unit to the top and bottom of the five-strip unit. Press.

Constructing the Project

1. Align the backing with the pieced block, right sides together. Mark a 2" section on the wrong side of the backing on the middle of the right side. Begin sewing at one end of the mark. Sew around the edges until you reach the beginning of the mark. Trim the corners. Turn inside out. Press.
2. Stuff with stuffing.
3. Sew red seed beads around the perimeter of the pin cushion. See "Beading" in the "Artistic Embellishments" chapter for instructions for sewing beads.
4. Sew a cowry shell in the center of the pin cushion, taking the thread through the whole pin cushion back up through the cowry shell at each end several times. Pull the thread as you sew to draw the pin cushion in at its middle. ❏

Fig. 1

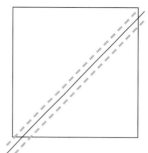

Two squares, right sides together, are stitched together then cut and pressed open.

Fig. 2

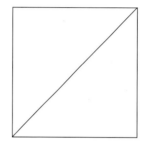

You will have two half square triangle blocks.

Fig. 3

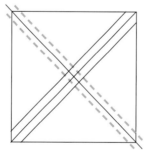

Place one half square triangle block and one solid square right sides together. Stitch, cut and press open.

Fig. 4

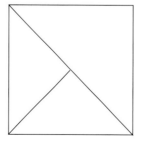

Two shadow blocks are completed.

Pieces needed

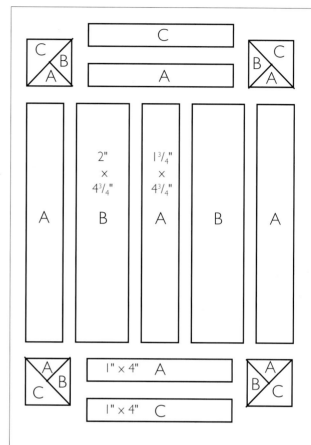

Finished Block

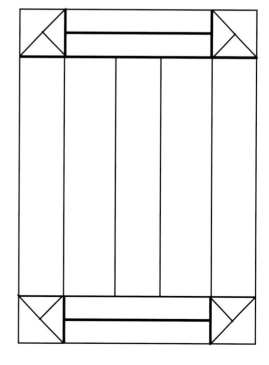

Nine Patch Pot Holders

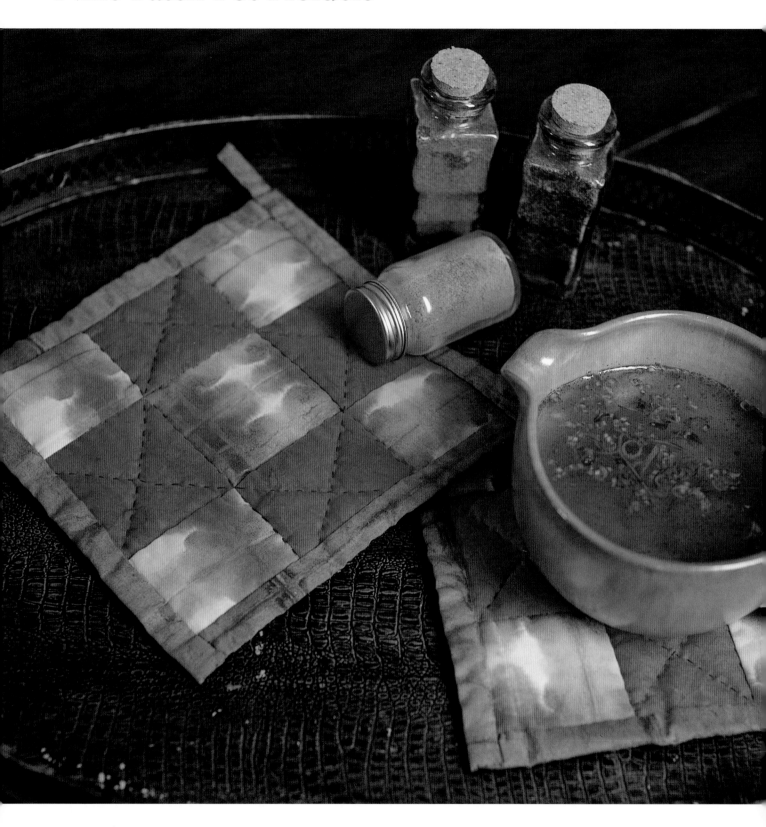

Instructions begin on page 78.

A

B

C

Nine Patch Pot Holders

These pot holders are a traditional quilt block pattern called a nine patch. Two fabrics, a multi-color tie dyed and an orange solid, were used for the nine-patch blocks. A brown tie-dyed fabric was used for the backing, which forms the binding, and for the hanger loops.

Pictured on page 77

Swatches of dyed fabric used to make this project, pictured top to bottom:
A – Multi-color (brown, orange, green, yellow) fan fold tie dyed
B – Orange solid hand dyed
C – Brown fan fold tie dyed

Pieces Needed for Block

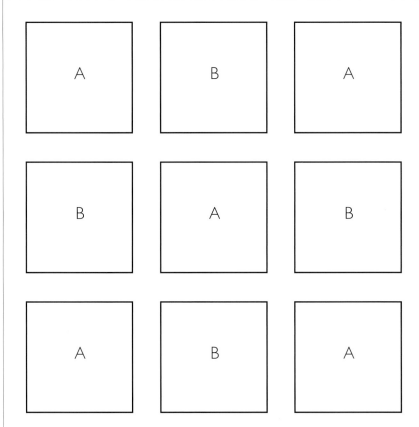

Components

For each pot holder

- Pieced block, 8" square
- Heat-resistant batting, 8¼" square
- Backing fabric, 10" square
- 100% cotton thread, matching color

Cutting the Fabric

1. From the multi-color fan fold tie-dyed fabric (A), cut:
   10 squares, each 3½".

2. From the orange solid fabric (B), cut:
   8 squares, each 3½".

3. From the brown tie-dyed fabric (C), cut:
   1 square, 10" (for the backing).
   1 strip, 1" x 2½" (for the hanger).

Piecing the Block

1. For each block, sew three rows of squares, alternating the colors. Use the project photo and the diagram as a guide. Press.
2. Sew the rows together to create a nine-patch block. Press.

Finished Block

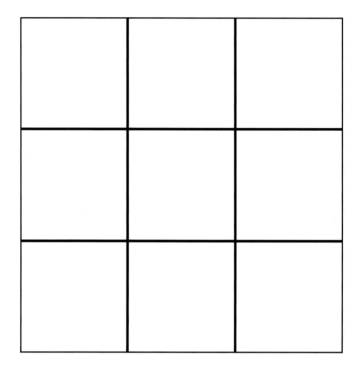

Constructing the Project

1. Make a quilt sandwich with the nine-patch block, batting, and backing, in that order. Center the block and the batting on the backing. Pin or needle baste.
2. Make hanger by turning each side of each strip over ¼". Fold strip in half and press. Sew along the open edge with small running stitches. Fold in half to create loop. Set aside.
3. Beginning on one side, sew all around the edge of the block to stabilize it, passing through all the layers.
4. Quilt-in-the-ditch along all seams.
5. Quilt an X on all orange squares.
6. Trim the batting even with the edge of the pieced block.
7. Trim the backing to 1" all around block.
8. Fold up the backing fabric ½" on all sides and finger press. Fold the remaining ½" of the backing fabric over the raw edges of the block. Finger press, pin in place, and tuck the two ends of hanger in the top corner. Pin to secure.
9. Blind stitch the binding on pot holder, taking care to backstitch the edges with the hanger. ❏

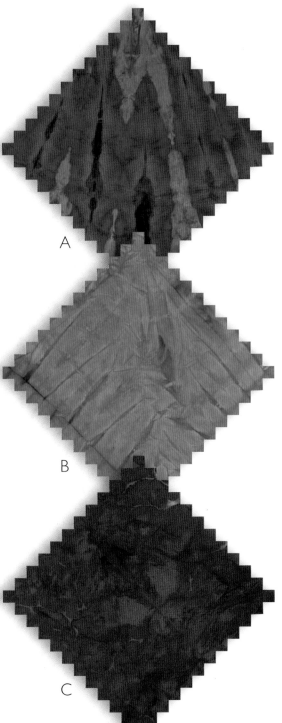

Beaded Blues Bookmark

This bookmark with beaded ends was created from two pieced quarter-square triangles and a blue square alternated with red-violet solid bars. Three different fabrics were used, and a piece of flannel is the batting.

Swatches of dyed fabric used to make this project, pictured top to bottom:
A – Blue & red-violet random line fold tie dyed
B – Blue fan fold tie dyed
C – Red-violet solid hand dyed

Components

- Pieced strip, 11" x 3"
- Flannel, 10" x 3"
- Backing fabric, 11" x 3"
- 100% cotton thread in a matching color
- Beads, two types, 5mm and 10mm

Cutting the Fabric

1. From the blue and red-violet tie dyed (A), cut:
   One 3" square.
   One 4" square.
   One piece, 10½" x 3¼" (for the backing).
2. From the blue tie-dyed fabric (B), cut:
   One 4" square.
3. From the red-violet solid fabric (C), cut:
   4 strips, each 1½" x 3".

Piecing the Block

Make the Quarter-Square Triangle Blocks:

1. On the back of the 4" blue and red-violet square, draw a pencil line on the diagonal from corner to corner. Place it over the blue tie-dyed square, align the edges, and sew ¼" from the line on both sides, back stitching as you begin and end. (Fig. 1)
2. Cut on the line and press with the seams on opposing sides. You now have two half-square triangle blocks. (Fig. 2)
3. Draw a diagonal line on one half-square triangle block perpendicular to the seam. Place it over the other half-square triangle block, aligning the seams. Sew ¼" from the line on both sides, back stitching as you begin and end. (Fig. 3)
4. Cut on the line and press. You now have two quarter-square triangle blocks. (Fig. 4)

continued on next page

Quarter Square Triangle

Fig. I

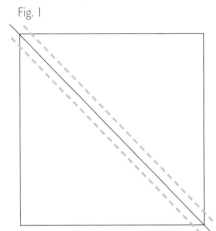

Fig. 2

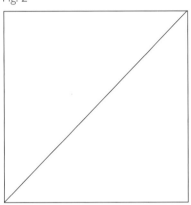

Fig. 3

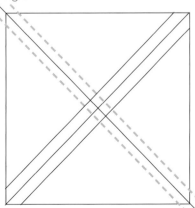

Fig. 4

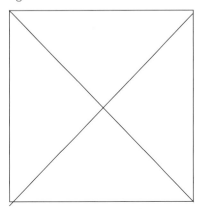

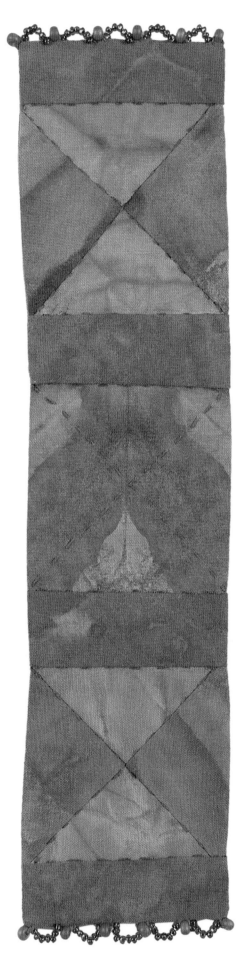

Beaded Blues Bookmark, continued

Make the Block:

1. Sew a red-violet bar to the top and bottom of each quarter square block to make two units. Press.
2. Sew the 3" tie-dyed square between the two units. Press.

Constructing the Project

1. Place the flannel in the center of the back side of the pieced block. (There should be at least ¼" of exposed fabric at each end.) Place this with right sides together on the backing piece.
2. With a sewing machine, stitch from top to bottom on both sides leaving the ends open. Trim the flannel back to the side seams.
3. Turn the bookmark inside out and press.
4. Tuck in the ¼" of fabric on each end. Press. Hand sew each end closed.
5. Quilt-in-the-ditch on all seams.
6. Sew beads on each end, using the photo as a guide. See "Beading" in the "Artistic Embellishments" chapter for instructions for sewing beads. ❑

Pieces Needed

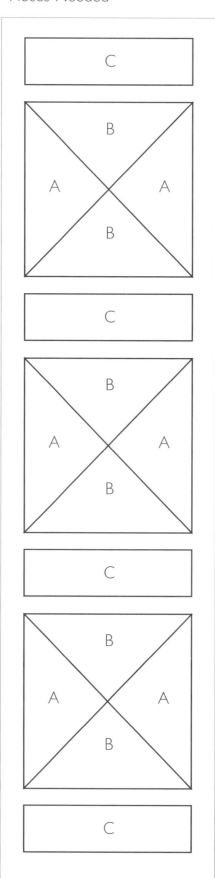

Finished Block

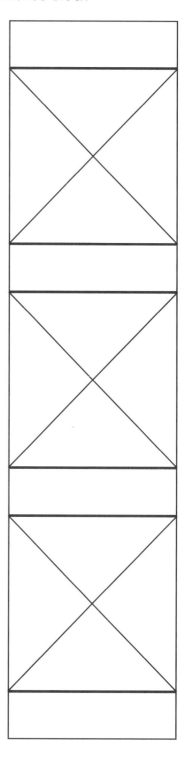

Triangles & Bars Hot or Cold Mat

Instructions begin on page 84.

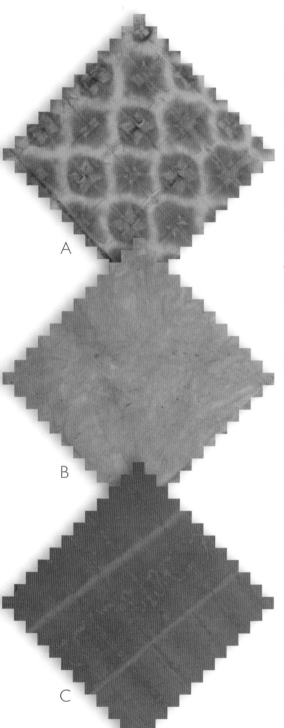

A

B

C

Triangles & Bars Hot or Cold Mat

Use this mat in the center of your dinner table to protect the table and provide a colorful centerpiece. After you make the quarter-square triangle block for the center, you'll have an identical one left over to use on another project or to make another mat.

Pictured on page 83

Swatches of dyed fabric used to make this project, pictured top to bottom:
A – Green and blue checkerboard fold tie dye
B – Green solid hand dyed
C – Red-orange fan fold tie dyed

Finished Block

Components

- Pieced block, 12" square
- Heat-resistant batting, 12½" square
- Backing fabric, 16" square
- 100% cotton thread in a matching color

Cutting the Fabric

1. From the green and blue tie-dyed (A), cut:
   One 8" square.
   Four 1½" x 7" strips.
2. From the green solid fabric (B), cut:
   Two 3" squares.
   Four 1½" x 7" strips.
3. From the red-orange tie-dyed fabric (C), cut:
   Two 3" squares.
   One 8" square.
   One 16" square (for the backing).

Piecing the Block

Make the Four Half-Square Triangle Blocks:

1. Draw a diagonal line on the wrong sides of the green 3" squares from corner to corner, using a pencil.
2. Place them, right sides together, on the red 3" squares and sew ¼" from the line on both sides, backstitching as you begin and end. (Fig. 1)
3. Cut on the line and press. You now have four half-square triangle blocks. (Fig. 2)

Make the Quarter-Square Triangle Block:

1. On the back of the 8" green and blue square, draw a pencil line on the diagonal from corner to corner.
2. Place it on the red 8" square and sew ¼" from the line on both sides, back stitching as you begin and end. (Fig. 1)
3. Cut on the line and press with the seams on opposing sides. You now have two half-square triangle blocks. (Fig. 2)
4. Draw a diagonal line on one half-square triangle block perpendicular

to the seam. Place it over the other half-square triangle block, aligning the seams. Sew ¼" from the line on both sides, back stitching as you begin and end. (Fig. 3)
5. Cut on the line and press. You now have two quarter-square triangle blocks. (Fig. 4) You'll use one for this project; save the other for another project.

Assemble the Block:

1. Sew the strips together in pairs (a green and blue one with a green one) to produce four strip sets. Press.
2. Sew a strip set to each side of the quarter-square block, using the photo as a guide for placement, to make the quarter-square set. Press.
3. Sew a small half-square triangle block to each end of the two remaining strip sets, creating longer strips. Press.

4. Sew the two longer strip sets to the top and bottom of the quarter-square set. Press.

Constructing the Project

1. Make a quilt sandwich with the pieced block, batting, and backing, in that order. Make sure the block and the batting are centered on the backing. Pin or needle baste.
2. Beginning on one side, sew all around the edge of the block to stabilize it, passing through all the layers.
3. Quilt-in-the-ditch along all seams.
4. Trim the batting to the edge of the quilt block.
5. Fold in the edges of the backing fabric ½" and finger press. Fold the remaining ½" of the fabric over the raw edges of the block to make the binding. Finger press and pin in place.
6. Sew the binding with a blind stitch. ❑

Half-Square Triangle Blocks

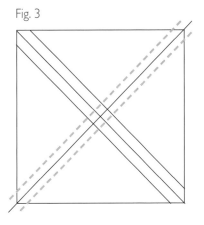

Fig. 1

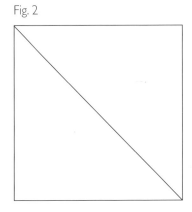

Fig. 2

Quarter-Square Triangle Blocks

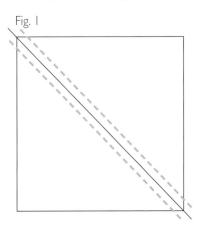

Fig. 3

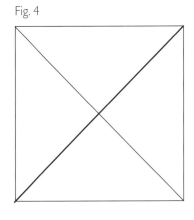

Fig. 4

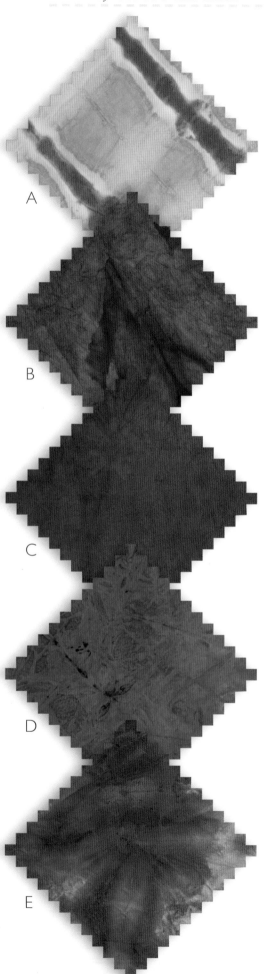

Maverick Block Quilt

Sometimes we deliberately choose to vary a quilt design and make a "mistake" in putting together a block. Though not readily apparent at first glance, a quilt with a few of these rearrangements can be more visually interesting and dynamic than a quilt that repeats itself with machine-like precision.

Swatches of dyed fabric used to make this project, pictured top to bottom:
A – Golden-yellow and brown fan fold tie dyed
B – Dark brown solid hand dyed
C – Rust solid hand dyed
D – Aqua solid hand dyed
E – Multi-colored (brown, aqua, gold) hand dyed

Instructions begin on page 88.

Maverick Block Quilt

Pictured on page 86

Components

■ Pieced top, 32½" x 41"

■ Batting, 33" x 41½"

■ Backing fabric, 38" x 46"

■ 100% cotton thread in a matching color

■ Seed beads, 4mm

■ Coconut shell beads

■ 4 flat copper beads

Cutting the Fabric

1. From the golden-yellow and brown tie dyed (A), cut:
   48 squares, each 2½".
   4 strips, 2" x width the fabric
   8 bars, each 3½" x 4½".
   14 bars, each 2" x 4½".

2. From the dark brown solid (B), cut:
   16 bars, 2" x 4½".

3. From the rust solid (C), cut:
   16 squares, each 5".

4. From the aqua solid (D), cut:
   16 squares, each 5".
   1 piece, 38" x 46" (for the backing).

5. From the multi-colored hand dyed (E), cut:
   48 squares, each 2½"
   10 bars, each 3" x 4½".

Piecing the Top

Make 24 Four-Patch Blocks:

1. Align a 2½" golden-yellow and brown tie dye square (A) and a 2½" multi-colored hand-dyed square (E). Sew a seam, creating a two-square unit. Press it with opposing seams to reduce bulk. Repeat the process to 48 two-square units.

2. Sew these units together with different colors facing each other to make 24 four-patch blocks.

Make 32 Half-Square Triangle Blocks:

1. Draw a diagonal line from corner to corner on the back of each of the 16 aqua 5" squares.

2. Place each, with right sides together, on a 5" rust square, aligning the edges. Sew ¼" from the drawn line on both sides, backstitching as you begin and end.

3. Cut on the line to make 32 half-square triangle squares in all.

Four-Patch Block

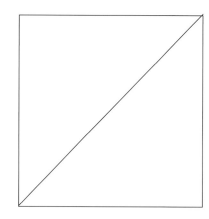

Half Square Triangle Block

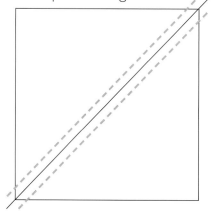

Place two solid squares right sides together. Stitch and cut.

Press open

Jacob's Ladder Block – Pieces Needed

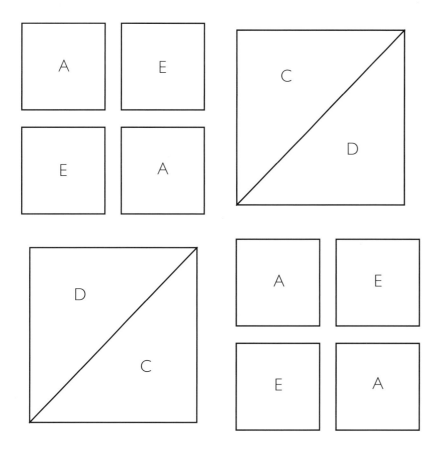

Make 12 Jacob's Ladder Blocks:

1. Make 11 Jacob's ladder blocks by taking 22 half-square triangle blocks and pairing them with 22 four-patch blocks. Align one of each type of block and sew a seam to create two units, each containing a four-patch block and a half-square triangle block. Press them with opposing seams to reduce bulk.
2. Sew pairs of units together so a four-patch block faces a half-square triangle block. Make 11 identical Jacob's ladder blocks. Press.
3. With the remaining two half-square triangle blocks and two four-patch blocks, make the maverick block, positioning the blocks as shown. Press.

Continued on next page

Finished Block – Jacob's Ladder

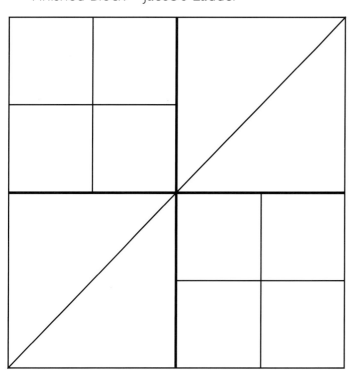

Finished Maverick Block

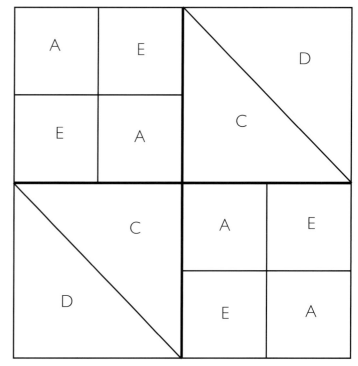

Assemble the Top:

1. Create four rows by sewing three Jacob's ladder blocks together. Place the maverick block in one of the rows to add visual interest. Press.

2. Sew the rows together to create a 12 block panel and press.

3. Sew a golden-yellow and brown tie-dyed 2" strip on the top and bottom of the 12 block panel. Trim and press.

4. Sew a 2" strip on each side. Trim excess and press. Set aside.

5. Create the borders on the two long sides by making two 41" mirror-image strips composed of two half-square triangle blocks and an assortment of the 4½" bars. Press.

6. Create the top and bottom borders by making two 32½" mirror-image strips composed of two half-square triangle blocks and an assortment of 4½" bars. Press.

7. Sew the 32½" border strips to the top and bottom of the 12 block panel.

8. Sew the 41" border strips to the sides. Press.

Constructing the Project

1. Make a quilt sandwich with the pieced top, batting, and backing, in that order. Make sure the top and batting are centered on the backing. Pin or needle baste.

2. Beginning on one side, sew all around the edge of the top to stabilize it, passing through all the layers.

3. Quilt-in-the-ditch along all the seams.

4. Trim the batting to the edge of the top.

5. Trim the backing to 1" all around the top.

6. Fold in the edges of the backing fabric ½" toward the top on all sides, finger pressing as you go. Fold the remaining ½" of the backing fabric over the raw edges of the quilt top. Finger press and pin in place on all sides.

7. Sew the binding in place with a blind stitch. ❑

Hills & Valleys Table Topper

Instructions begin on page 92

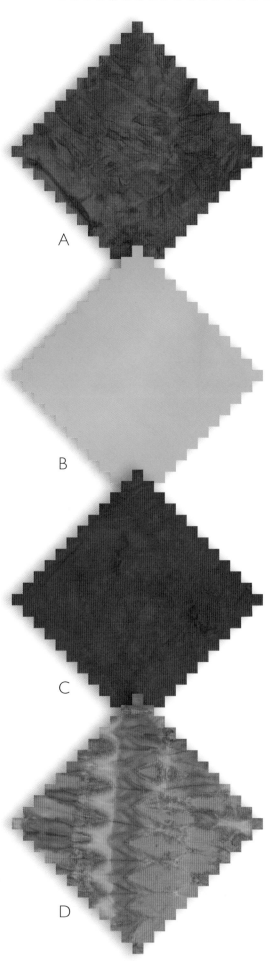

Hills & Valleys Table Topper

Half-square triangle blocks in different color combinations create the central block, which is framed by a simple border.

Swatches of dyed fabric used to make this project, pictured top to bottom:
A – Blue and purple hand dyed
B – Light blue solid hand dyed
C – Purple solid hand dyed
D – Multi-color (orange, blue, purple) random line fold tie dyed

Components

- Pieced top, 23" x 25"
- Batting, 23" x 25"
- Backing fabric, 26" x 28"
- 100% cotton thread in a matching color

Cutting the Fabric

1. From the blue and purple hand dyed (A), cut:
   2 strips, each 4" x 23".
   2 strips, each 4" x 18½".
   1 piece, 26" x 28" (for the backing).

2. From light blue solid (B), cut:
   5 squares, each 4".

3. From purple solid (C), cut:
   5 squares, each 4".

4. From the multi-color tie dyed (D), cut:
   10 squares, each 4".

Piecing the Block

Make the Half-Square Triangle Blocks:

1. On all 10 of the 4" multi-color tie dye squares, use a pencil to draw a line on the diagonal from corner to corner on the wrong side of the fabric.
2. Pair each one, right sides together, with the light blue 4" squares (B) and the purple 4" squares (C). Align the edges and sew ¼" from the line on both sides, backstitching as you begin and end. (See Fig. 1)
3. Cut each one on the line – you will have two half-square triangle blocks. Press them toward the tie-dyed side. Continue until you have completed 20 in all. (See Fig. 2)

Assemble the Top:

1. Create a row, each consisting of four blocks, alternating between the light blue and purple. Press the seams. Repeat four times to make five rows.
2. Sew the rows together to create the center block of half-square blocks. Press the seams. (See Fig. 3)
3. On the bottom and top of the center block, sew a 4" x 18½" blue and purple border strip (A). Press the seams.
4. On the sides, sew the 4" x 23" blue and purple border strips (A). Press the seams.

Constructing the Project

1. Make a quilt sandwich with the pieced top, batting, and backing, in that order. Make sure the top and the batting are centered on the backing. Pin or needle baste.
2. Beginning on one side, sew all around the edge of the top to stabilize it, passing through all the layers.
3. Quilt-in-the-ditch along all seams. Quilt the border, as desired.
4. Trim the batting to the edge of the pieced top.
5. Fold in the edges of the backing fabric ½" toward the top on all sides, finger pressing as you go. Fold the remaining ½" of the backing fabric over the raw edges of the quilt top. Finger press and pin in place on all sides.
6. Sew the binding in place with a blind stitch. ❑

Half Square Triangle Blocks

Fig. 1

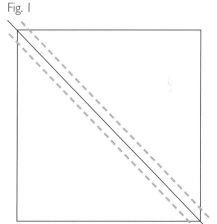

Place two solid squares rights sides together. Stitch and cut on the line drawn.

Fig. 2

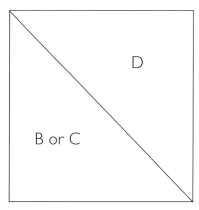

Press open.

Fig. 3

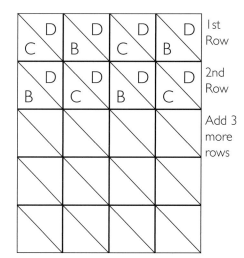

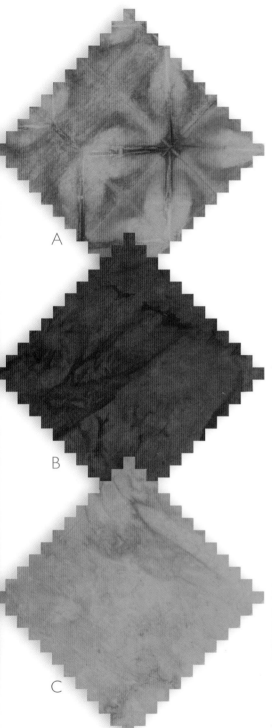

Sky & Meadow Floor Pillow

The blues and greens of the three fabrics evoke the colors of the earth and sky. The blocks are made from bars and strips, and piecing them is easy.

Swatches of dyed fabric used to make this project, pictured top to bottom:
A – Blue and green envelope fold tie dyed
B – Blue-violet solid hand dyed
C – Green solid hand dyed

Instructions begin on page 96.

Sky & Meadow Floor Pillow

Pictured on page 94

Components

- Pieced top, 28½" x 32"
- Batting, 29" x 32½"
- 2 pieces backing fabric, each 28½" x 18"
- 100% cotton thread in a matching color
- Plain muslin, 29" x 32½" (for interior backing of top)
- 3 large bags of stuffing
- 2 pieces muslin, 28" x 31½" (to make the pillow form)

Cutting the Fabrics

1. From the blue and green tie-dyed fabric (A), cut:
   5 strips, each 2½" x the width of the fabric.

2. From the blue-violet solid fabric (B), cut:
   5 strips, each 2½" x the width of the fabric.
   6 strips, each 2½" x 6".

3. From the green solid fabric (C), cut:
   5 strips, each 2½" x the width of the fabric.

Piecing the Pillow Top

1. Create five three-strip sets with one strip of each of the three fabrics. Press. (See Fig. 1)
2. To create a Perpendicular Bar Set, cut three pieces 6" long from one of the three-strip sets. On one of them, sew a 2½" x 6" strip of blue-violet across the top and bottom. Press. Sew the other two 6" units on each side of this bar set. Press. (See Fig. 2) Repeat to make two more Perpendicular Bar Sets.
3. From the remaining three-strip sets, cut two 20½" units and two 28½" units. Press.
4. Assemble the top by sewing a 20½" unit between the Perpendicular Bar Sets. (This will create a pieced block with five sections.) Press.
5. Sew a 28½" unit from the three-strip sets to each side of the five-section pieced block. Press.

Constructing the Project

Make the Cover:

1. Make a quilt sandwich with the pillow top, batting, and muslin interior backing, in that order. Make sure the top and batting are centered on the backing. Pin or needle baste.
2. Beginning on one side, sew all around the edge of the top to stabilize it, passing through all layers.
3. Quilt-in-the-ditch along the seams. When finished, trim the backing and batting to the edge of the pillow top.
4. On the two pieces of the backing fabric, make a ½" fold along the top of the 28½" sides on both pieces. Finger press and fold over ½" again. Sew and press.
5. Overlap the hemmed edges as you place them, right sides facing with the right side of the top. Pin in place, making sure the backing pieces overlap each other at least 2".
6. Sew all around the pillow top, taking out the pins as you go.
7. Trim the edges of the seams and clip the corners. Turn the pillow cover inside out through the back overlap. Press the edges and set the pillow cover aside.

Make the Pillow Form:

1. On one of the two 28" x 31½" pieces of muslin, draw a 4" line ¼" from the top in the middle of the wrong side. Place the other piece of muslin under it, right sides together. Starting at one end of the marked line, sew around the edges until you reach the beginning of the line and backstitch at the end.
2. Turn inside out. Press.
3. Stuff the pillow form. Sew up the opening.
4. Insert the form in the pillow cover. ❑

Fig. 1
Three-Bar Sets

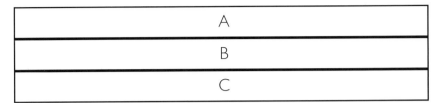

Fig. 2
Perpendicular Bar Sets

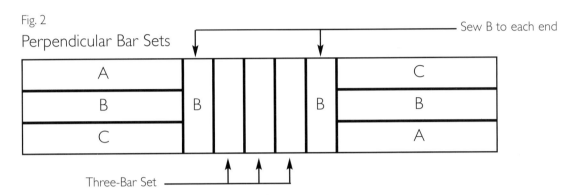

Finished Top

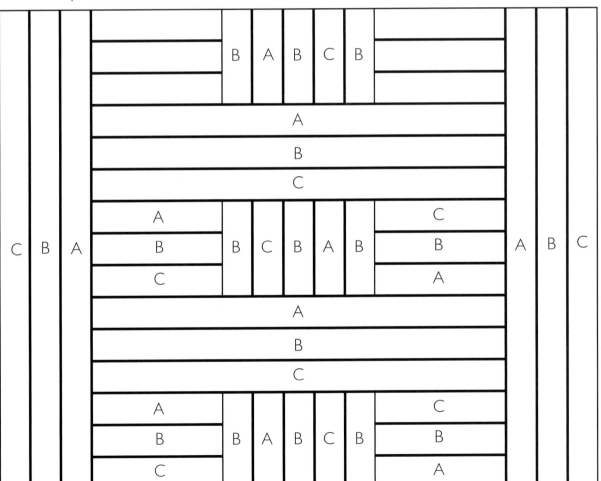

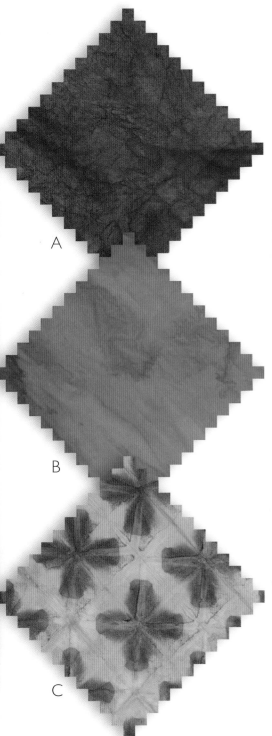

House Top Pillow

The house top quilt block begins with a central square. Bars and strips of fabric are added on alternating opposing sides to create the square house top block. This one is made from three fabrics. The central square is embellished with a cowry shell.

Swatches of dyed fabric used to make this project, pictured top to bottom:
A – Brown solid hand dyed
B – Turquoise blue solid hand dyed
C – Multi-color (turquoise blue, yellow, brown) triangle fold tie dyed

Instructions begin on page 100.

House Top Pillow

Pictured on page 98

Components

- Pieced top, 23" square
- Batting, 23½" square
- 2 pieces backing fabric, each 23½" x 17"
- 100% cotton thread in a matching color
- 2 large bags stuffing
- 1 piece muslin, 23½" square (for the interior backing of the top)
- 2 pieces muslin, each 24" square (to create the pillow form)
- 1 large cowry shell

Cutting the Fabrics

1. From the brown solid fabric (A), cut:
   2 bars, each 1" x 5".
   2 bars, each 1" x 6¼".
   2 bars, each 1½" x 8".
   2 bars, each 1½" x 10".
   2 strips, each 1½" x 17".
   2 strips, each 1½" x 19½".
   10 bars, each 2" x 2½".

2. From the turquoise blue solid fabric (B), cut:
   2 bars, each 1½" x 6".
   2 bars, each 1½" x 8".
   2 bars, each 2" x 10".
   2 strips, each 2" x 13½".
   2 strips, each 2½" x 19".
   2 strips, each 2½" x 23".
   10 bars, each 2½" x 3".

3. From the multi-color tie-dyed fabric (C), cut:
   1 square, 5".
   10 squares, each 2½".

Piecing the Top

Make the House Top Block:

The house top block starts with a square. Pairs of bars or strips are added to opposite sides in succession to build the block.

1. Take the 5" multi-color square (C) and sew the 1" x 5" brown bars (A) on the top and bottom of it. Press. Sew the 1" x 6¼" brown bars to the sides. Press.
2. Sew the two 1½" x 6" turquoise blue bars (B) to the top and bottom. Press. Sew the two 1½" x 8" turquoise blue bars to the sides.
3. Sew the 2½" x 8" brown bars to the top and bottom. Press. Sew the 1½" x 10" brown bars to the sides. Press.
4. Sew the two 2" x 10" turquoise blue bars to the top and bottom. Press. Sew the two 2" x 13½" turquoise blue strips to the sides. Press and set aside.

Make the Inner Border:

1. Create two 12½" x 2½" strips by sewing two 2" x 2½" brown bars, two 2½" x 3" turquoise blue bars, and three 2½" multi-color squares together, alternating the colors. Press.
2. Sew to the top and bottom of the house top block. Press.
3. Create two 2½" x 17½" strips by sewing two 2" x 2½" brown bars, three 2½" multi-color squares, and four 2½" x 3" turquoise blue bars together, alternating the colors. Press.
4. Sew to the sides of the house top block. Press.

Add the Solid-Color Outer Borders:

1. Sew the two 1½" x 17" brown strips to the top and bottom. Press.
2. Sew the two 1½" x 19½" brown strips to the sides. Press.
3. Sew the two 2½" x 19" turquoise blue strips to the top and bottom. Press.
4. Complete the pillow top by sewing the two 2½" x 23" turquoise blue strips to the sides. Press.

Constructing the Project

Make the Pillow Cover:

1. Make a quilt sandwich with the pillow top, batting, and muslin interior backing, in that order. Pin or needle baste.
2. Beginning on one side, sew all around the edge of the top to stabilize it, passing through all the layers.
3. Quilt-in-the-ditch along the seams.
4. Quilt an X in the center square.
5. When finished, trim the backing and batting to the edge of the pillow top.
6. Sew the cowry shell in the center in the middle of the X.
7. Take the two pieces of the backing fabric. Make a ½" fold along the top of the 23½" side on both pieces. Finger press and fold over ½" again. Sew. Press.
8. Overlap the hemmed edges as you place them with right sides facing the right side of the top. Pin in place, making sure the backing pieces overlap at least 2".
9. Sew all around the Pillow Top taking out the pins as you go.
10. Trim the edges and clip the corners. Turn the pillow cover inside out through the back overlap. Press the edges and set the pillow cover aside.

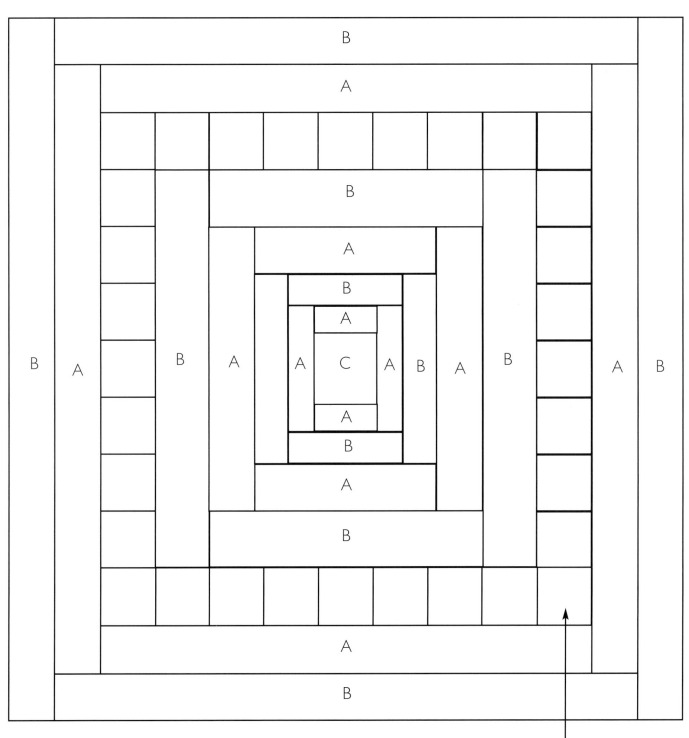

ABC in various
combinations

Make the Pillow Form:

1. On one of the two 24" square pieces of muslin, draw a 4" line ¼" from the
   top in the middle of the wrong side. Place the other piece of muslin under
   it, right sides together. Starting at one end of the marked line, sew around
   the edges until you reach the beginning of the line and backstitch at the end.
2. Turn inside out. Press.
3. Stuff the pillow form. Sew up the opening.
4. Insert the form in the pillow cover. ❏

A

B

C

D

E   F

Jazzy Checkerboard Quilt

This quilt top is composed of 25 blocks, each 5½" square. Six fabrics were used to construct the quilt, which is decorated with beads.

Swatches of dyed fabric used to make this project, pictured top to bottom:
A – Blue random line fold tie dyed
B – Blue and yellow multiple circle fold tie dyed
C – Multi-color (blue, orange, yellow) hand dyed
D – Red solid hand dyed
E – Dark blue solid hand dyed
F – Green solid hand dyed

Instructions begin on page 104.

Jazzy Checkerboard Quilt

Pictured on page 102

Components

- Pieced top, 26" square (composed of 25 blocks)
- Batting, 26½" square
- Backing fabric, 30" square
- 100% cotton thread of a matching color
- 8 faceted glass beads
- 14 glass seed beads, 5mm

Cutting the Fabric

1. From the blue tie-dyed fabric (A), cut:
   3 strips, each 2" x 20".
   1 square, 30" (for the backing).

2. From the blue and yellow circle fold tie-dyed fabric (B), cut:
   12 squares, each 4½".

3. From the multi-color hand-dyed fabric (C), cut:
   2 strips, each 2" x 20".

4. From the red solid fabric (D), cut:
   10 strips, each 1½" x 4½".
   10 strips, each 1½" x 5½".
   3 strips, each 2" x 20".

5. From the dark blue solid fabric (E), cut:
   2 strips, each 1½" x 4½".
   4 strips, each 2" x 20".

6. From the green solid fabric (F), cut:
   4 strips, each 2" x 20".

Checkerboard Blocks

Fig. 1

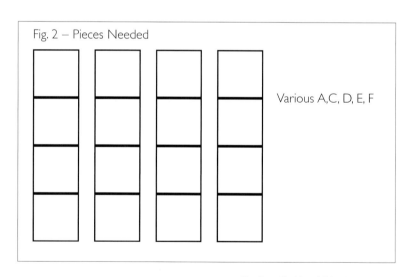

Sew 4 strips together to make one strip set

Make 4 strip sets

← Cut 1½" strips across seams

Fig. 2 – Pieces Needed

Various A, C, D, E, F

Fig. 3 – Finished Block

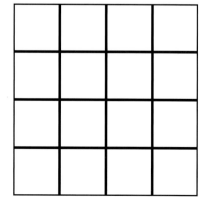

Piecing the Top

Make the Checkerboard Blocks:

1. Make four strip sets with the 2" x 20" strips, using four strips for each set, sewing them together lengthwise. (Fig. 1) The color choices are up to you. TIP: When sewing the strips together, alternate the end you begin sewing from to minimize distortion.
2. Cut each set across the seams into 1½" units of four squares. (Fig. 1)
3. Lay out four units in a pleasing pattern and sew them together, creating a block with 16 squares that measures 5½" square. Press. Repeat this process, creating 13 blocks in all. (Figs. 2 and 3)

Make the Two-Piece Blocks:

1. Sew a blue 4½" strip (E) to one side of a circle fold tie-dyed square (B).
2. Make two of these blocks. Press.

Make the Three-Piece Blocks:

1. Sew a red 4½" strip (D) to one side of a 4½" square (B). Make 10 units.
2. Sew a 5½" red strip (D) on one side of 10 units made previously in such a way that five of them mirror the other five. Press all seams.

Assemble the Top:

1. Lay out the blocks in five horizontal rows in an alternating grid, using the photo as a guide. Place the two Two-Piece Blocks on rows two and four, facing each other as shown.
2. Sew horizontal rows composed of five blocks. Press.
3. Sew the rows together and press. This will create a 26" square top.

Constructing the Project

1. Make a quilt sandwich with the quilt top, batting, and backing, in that order. Make sure the quilt top and batting are centered on the backing. Pin or needle baste.
2. Beginning on one side, sew all around the edge of the quilt top to stabilize it, passing through all the layers.
3. Quilt-in-the-ditch along all the seams.
4. Quilt an X on each circle fold tie-dyed square.
5. Trim the edges of the batting even with the edges of the quilt top.
6. Trim the backing to 1" all around the quilt top.
7. Fold in the edges of the backing fabric ½" toward the top on all sides, finger pressing as you go. Fold the remaining ½" of the backing fabric over the raw edges of the quilt top. Finger press and pin in place on all sides.
8. Sew the binding in place with a blind stitch.
9. Add beaded embellishments to the blue bars strips to complete the quilt. See "Beading" in the Artistic Embellishments chapter. ❏

Two-Piece Block
Pieces Needed

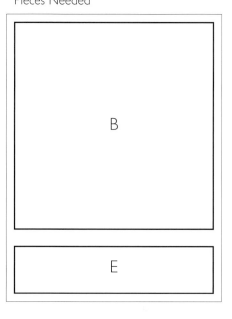

Finished Block

Three-Piece Block
Pieces Needed

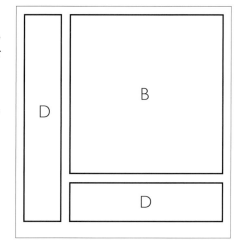

Rail Fence Quilt

This quilt top is composed of twelve 8"
blocks. It was created with six fabrics.
Just add additional blocks to make a
bigger quilt.

*Swatches of dyed fabric used to make this project, pictured
top to bottom:*
A – Dark brown solid hand dyed
B – Tan solid hand dyed
*C – Brick red solid hand dyed (1 part dark brown/
    3 parts red)*
D – Black solid hand dyed
E – Cream solid hand dyed
F – Multi-color (gray, silver, gold) drop painted

Instructions begin on page 108

Rail Fence Quilt

Pictured on page 106

Components

- Pieced top, 32½" x 28½" (composed of twelve 8" blocks)
- Batting, 29½" x 25½"
- Backing fabric, 34" x 30", brick red solid
- 100% cotton thread of a matching color

Cutting the Fabric

1. From the dark brown solid fabric (A), cut:
   7 strips, each 1½" x 8½".
   7 strips, each 1½" x 7½".

2. From the tan solid fabric (B), cut:
   8 strips, each 2½" x 10".
   12 strips, each 2½" x 8½".
   4 strips, each 1½" x 7½".
   2 strips, each 1½" x 8½".

3. From the brick red solid fabric (C), cut:
   7 strips, each 1½" x 8½".
   7 strips, each 1½" x 7½".

4. From the black solid fabric (D), cut:
   8 strips, each 2½" x 10".
   12 strips, each 2½" x 8½".
   4 strips, each 1½" x 8½".
   4 strips, each 1½" x 7½".

5. From the cream solid fabric (E), cut:
   12 strips, each 1½" x 7½".

6. From the multi-color drop painted fabric (F), cut:
   4 strips, each 1½" x 8½".
   6 strips, each 1½" x 7½".

Piecing the Top

Create the Strip Sets A:
(See Fig. 1)

1. Sew 8 of the 1½"x 7½" strips together. Use assorted colors. Sew the long sides of the strips together, alternating the end you begin sewing from to minimize distortion.
2. Repeat Step 1 four more times to make a total of 5 eight-strip sets.
3. Cut the eight-strip sets into strips 1½" wide across the seams. These are the A strip sets for the pieced rails. You will need 24 sets.

Create the Strip Sets B:
(See Fig. 2)

1. Make 8 strip sets composed of:
   1 strip of tan (B) 2½" x 10", and 1 strip 2½" x 10" of black (D). Sew the long sides of the strips together, alternating the end you begin sewing from to minimize distortion.
2. Cut the two-strip sets into pieces 2½" wide across the seams. Sew the 2½" strips together end to end, with 16 squares in each strip, making two strips. Press and set aside.

Make the Rail Fence Blocks:
(See Fig. 3)

1. Sew together lengthwise, in this order:
   1 tan strip 2½" x 8½" (B)
   1 strip set A
   1 strip, 1½" x 8½" (color of your choice)
   1 strip set A section
   1 black strip (D), 2½" x 8½"
   1 strip, 1½" x 8½" (color of your choice).
   This will create one rail fence block.
2. Repeat this process to create a total of 12 rail fence blocks.

Assemble the Top:

1. Create three vertical rows of rail fence blocks, using the photo as a guide and putting four blocks in each row. Alternate the directions of the rails so that some are vertical and others are horizontal. Press.
2. Sew the rows of rail fence blocks together, separated by the strip sets B. This will create the quilt top.

Constructing the Project

1. Make a quilt sandwich with the quilt top, batting, and backing, in that order. Make sure the quilt top and batting are centered on the backing. Pin or needle baste.
2. Beginning on one side, sew all around the edge of the quilt top to stabilize it, passing through all the layers.
3. Quilt-in-the-ditch along all the seams.
4. Trim the edges of the batting even with the edges of the quilt top.
5. Trim the backing to 1" all around the quilt top.
6. Fold in the edges of the backing fabric ½" toward the top on all sides, finger pressing as you go. Fold the remaining ½" of the backing fabric over the raw edges of the quilt top. Finger press and pin in place on all sides.
7. Blind stitch the binding in place. ❑

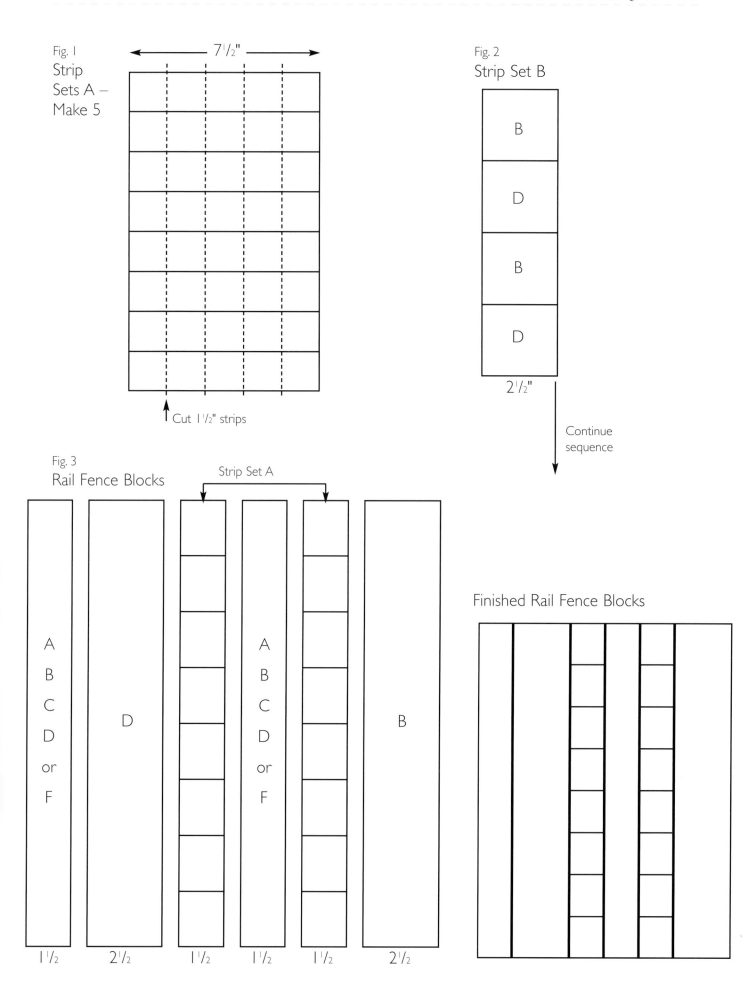

Fig. 1
Strip
Sets A –
Make 5

7¹/₂"

Cut 1¹/₂" strips

Fig. 2
Strip Set B

B

D

B

D

2¹/₂"

Continue
sequence

Fig. 3
Rail Fence Blocks

Strip Set A

A
B
C
D
or
F

D

A
B
C
D
or
F

B

1¹/₂   2¹/₂   1¹/₂   1¹/₂   1¹/₂   2¹/₂

Finished Rail Fence Blocks

Marquetta 2006 ©

Blue Blossoms Quilt

The three yo-yo blossoms on this quilt bloom
from a pieced checkerboard flower pot.
The flowers, leaves, stems, and flowerpot
were appliqued to the quilt top. It was
created with six fabrics.

*Swatches of dyed fabric used to make this project, pictured
top to bottom:*
A – Red-violet and blue random line fold tie dyed
B – Red-violet solid hand dyed
C – Blue-violet solid hand dyed
D – Light blue solid hand dyed
E – Green solid hand dyed
F – Dark blue and blue fan fold tie dyed

Instructions begin on page 112

Blue Blossoms Quilt

Pictured on page 110

Components

- Pieced top, 12½" x 24"
- 3 yo-yos
- 5 fabric leaf shapes lined with interfacing
- 1 pieced flower pot
- 3 fabric flower stems, ½" wide
- Medium weight interfacing, 4½" x 5½"
- Batting, 14" x 24½"
- Backing fabric, 18" x 28"
- 100% cotton thread of a matching color

Cutting the Fabric

1. From red-violet and blue tie dyed (A), cut:
   2 bars, each 1½" x 8"
   1 piece, 5" x 9"
   3 circles, each 6" diameter

2. From red-violet solid (B), cut:
   1 bar, 1½" x 8".
   1 piece, 9" x 15".

3. From the blue-violet solid (C), cut:
   1 bar, 1½" x 8".

4. From light blue solid (D), cut:
   1 bar, 1½" x 8".

5. From the green solid fabric (E), cut:
   3 stems according to pattern.
   5 leaf shapes according to pattern.

6. From dark blue and blue tie dyed (F), cut:
   1 bar, 1½" x 8".

7. From all the fabrics (A, B, C, D, E, and F), cut:
   60 bars, each 2" x 3", in various colors.

Piecing the Top

Make the Flower Pot Applique:

(See Fig. 1)

1. Sew a strip set with the six 1½" x 8" bars of the various colors. Press.
2. Cut across the seams to make five sections, 1½" wide.
3. Arrange the sections to make a checkerboard design, staggering the seam placement of the strips a little, a lot, or not at all. Sew them together. Press.
4. Using the flower pot pattern, cut out the shape from the checkerboard piece and the 4½" x 5½" piece of interfacing.
5. Place the two pattern pieces right sides together and sew all the way around the flower pot.
6. Carefully cut a slit in the middle of the back. Turn the pot inside out. Press. Set aside.

Make the Flowers & Leaves Appliques:

1. Make the stems by folding the three green strips in half and sewing ¼" from the edges from top to bottom.
2. Press the strips with the seams on the back. Put these aside.
3. Using the pattern provided, cut out five leaf shapes from interfacing. Align each with a green fabric leaf shape, placing them right sides together. Sew around the curved edges of each one. Clip the seams. Turn them inside out, press, and put them aside.
4. With the red-violet and blue tie-dyed circles, make the yo-yos. See "Yo-yos" in the "Artistic Embellishments" chapter.

continued on page 114

Fig. 1

Flower Pot Applique Block

6-strip set

Cut 1½" across seamed strips

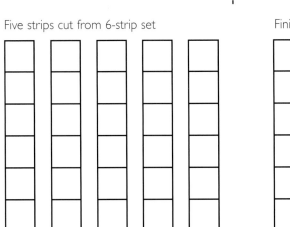

Five strips cut from 6-strip set

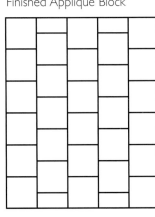

Finished Applique Block

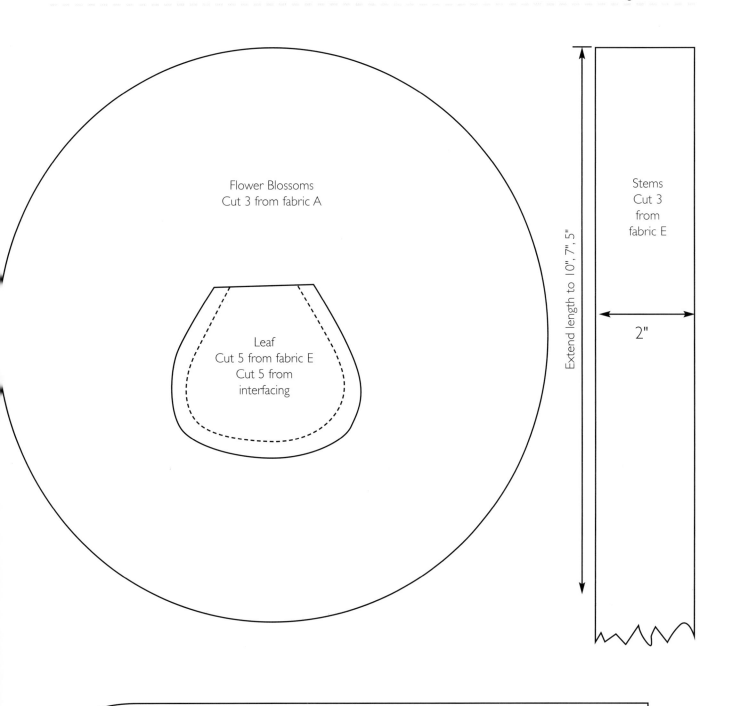

Flower Blossoms
Cut 3 from fabric A

Leaf
Cut 5 from fabric E
Cut 5 from
interfacing

Stems
Cut 3
from
fabric E

Extend length to 10", 7", 5"

2"

Flower Pot
Cut from checkerboard
pieced block

Place on Fold

continued from page 112

Make the Two-Color Bars:

1. Make six two-color bars with six pairs of 2" x 3" bars: Place them perpendicular and overlapping, right sides together, and sew a seam across the corner at a 45 degree angle. Trim the seam. Press open.
2. Trim the two-color bars to 2" x 3".

Make Borders:

Sew all the 2" x 3" bars together to make two 24½" strips and two 9" strips. Place the two-color bars randomly along strips. Sew along the 3" side. Press.

Assemble the Quilt Top:

1. Sew all the 9" sides of the 9" x 15" red-violet fabric piece and the 5" x 9" red-violet and blue tie-dyed fabric piece together to make the central block. Press.
2. Sew the 9" bar strips to the 9" ends of the central block.
3. Sew the 24½" bar strips to the long sides. Press.
4. Using the photo as a guide for placement, arrange and pin the pot, stems, leaves, and flower blossoms on the central block. Sew them in place with blind stitches.

Constructing the Project

1. Make a quilt sandwich with the quilt top, batting, and backing, in that order. Make sure the quilt top and batting are centered on the backing. Pin or needle baste.
2. Beginning on one side, sew all around the edge of the quilt top to stabilize it, passing through all the layers.
3. Quilt-in-the-ditch along all the seams.
4. Make tacking stitches in the face of the quilt.
5. Quilt around the appliques on the central block.
6. When the quilting is finished, trim the batting even with the edges of the quilt top.
7. Trim the backing to 1" all around the quilt top.
8. Fold in the edges of the backing fabric ½" toward the top on all sides, finger pressing as you go. Fold the remaining ½" of the backing fabric over the raw edges of the quilt top. Finger press and pin in place on all sides.
9. Blind stitch the binding in place. ❑

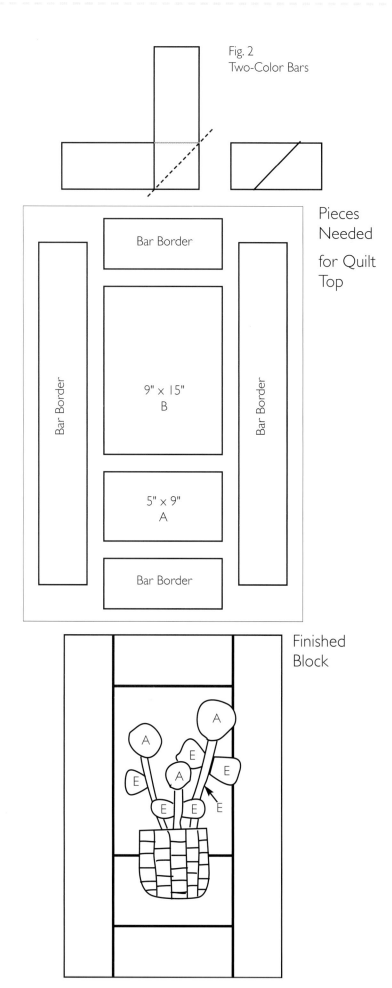

Fig. 2
Two-Color Bars

Pieces
Needed

for Quilt
Top

Finished
Block

Color Wheel Checkerboard Drop Painted Quilt

Instructions begin on page 116.

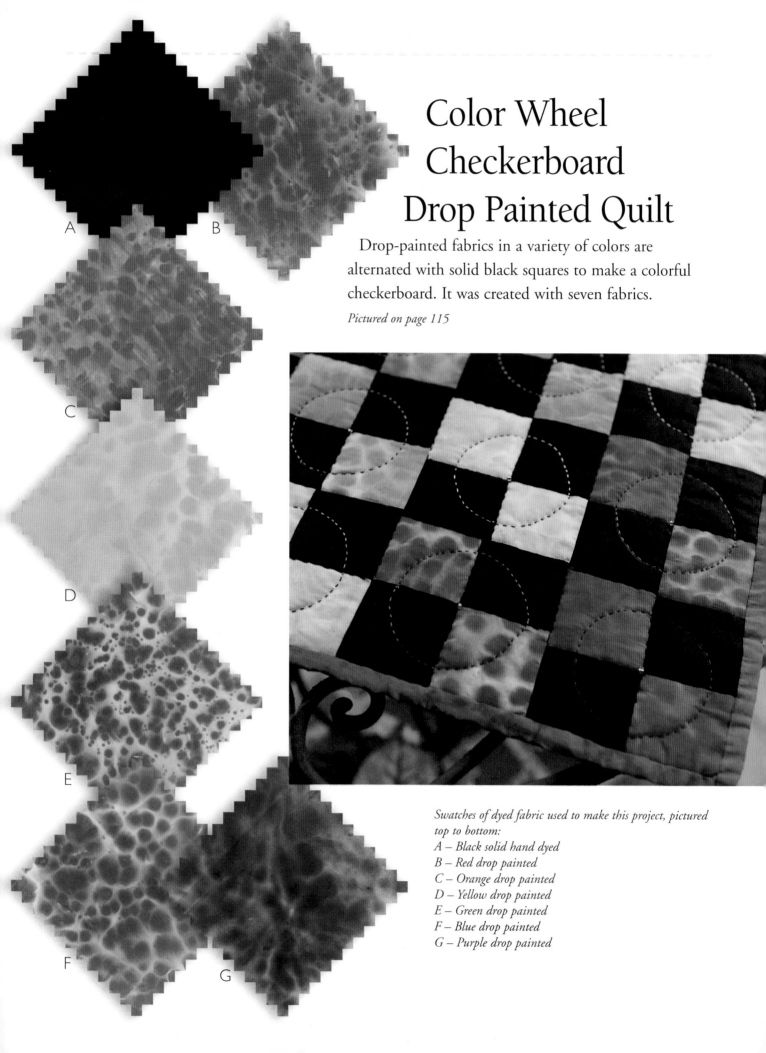

Color Wheel Checkerboard Drop Painted Quilt

Drop-painted fabrics in a variety of colors are alternated with solid black squares to make a colorful checkerboard. It was created with seven fabrics.

Pictured on page 115

Swatches of dyed fabric used to make this project, pictured top to bottom:
A – Black solid hand dyed
B – Red drop painted
C – Orange drop painted
D – Yellow drop painted
E – Green drop painted
F – Blue drop painted
G – Purple drop painted

Components

- Pieced top, 34½" square
- Batting, 35" square
- Backing fabric, 39" square (any single color)
- 100% cotton thread of a matching color
- Embroidery floss – Red, orange, yellow, green, blue, purple
- Seed beads, 4mm

Cutting the Fabric

1. From the black solid fabric (A), cut:

   72 squares, each 3½".

2. From the red drop painted fabric (B), cut:

   4 squares, each 3½".

3. From the orange drop painted fabric (C), cut:

   8 squares, each 3½".

4. From the yellow drop painted fabric (D), cut:

   12 squares, each 3½".

5. From the green drop painted fabric (E), cut:

   16 squares, each 3½".

6. From the blue drop painted fabric (F), cut:

   20 squares, each 3½".

7. From the purple drop painted fabric (G), cut:

   12 squares, each 3½".

Piecing the Top

1. Make 36 four-patch blocks, using two same-color drop painted squares and two black squares. Align a back square and a colored square and sew a seam to create two units with two squares. Press open the seams to reduce bulk. Sew two units with the same color together, using the diagram as a guide, to create a four-patch unit. Press them.
2. Sew rows of six four-patch blocks together, using the photo and diagrams as guides for placement. Press. TIP: Lay them out on the floor or on your design wall.
3. Sew the rows together to make the quilt top. Press.

Constructing the Project

1. Make a quilt sandwich with the quilt top, batting, and backing, in that order. Make sure the quilt top and batting are centered on the backing. Pin or needle baste.
2. Beginning on one side, sew all around the edge of the quilt top to stabilize it, passing through all the layers.
3. Quilt-in-the-ditch along all the seams.
4. On each four-patch block, quilt a 3¾" diameter circle. Use floss that matches the color of the drop painted fabric squares.
5. Sew a 4mm bead in the center of each circle.
6. Trim the edges of the batting even with the edges of the quilt top.
7. Trim the backing so it extends 1" beyond the quilt top on all sides.
8. Fold in the edges of the backing fabric ½" toward the top on all sides, finger pressing as you go. Fold the remaining ½" of the backing fabric over the raw edges of the quilt top. Finger press and pin in place on all sides.
9. Blind stitch the binding in place. ❏

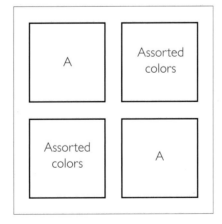

Four-Patch Block – Pieces Needed

Finished Block

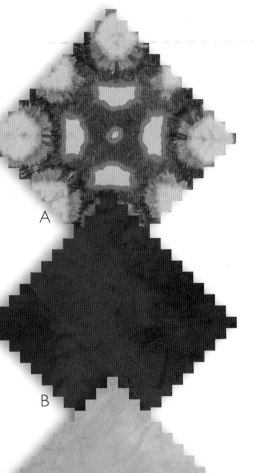

Appliqued Circles Quilt

This quilt was created with six fabrics. It is pieced from bars and pinwheel blocks, and decorated with appliqued circles.

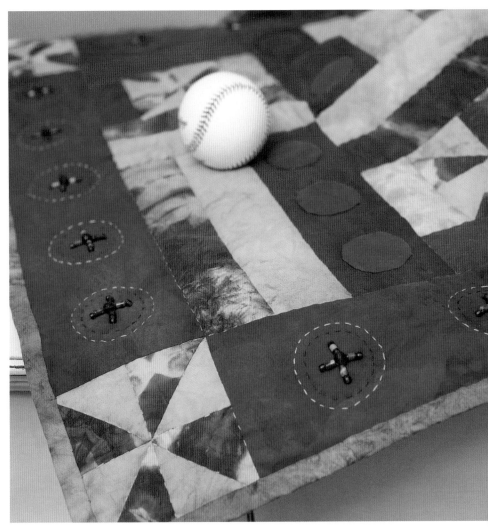

Swatches of dyed fabric used to make this project, pictured top to bottom:
A – Multi-color (red, yellow, blue) mandala fold tie dyed
B – Dark blue solid hand dyed
C – Light green solid hand dyed
D – Red solid hand dyed
E – Multi-color (red, yellow, blue) spiral fold tie dyed
F – Golden yellow drop painted

Instructions begin on page 120.

Appliqued Circles Quilt

Pictured on page 118

Components

- Pieced top, 22½" x 27½"
- Batting, 23" x 28"
- Backing fabric, 28" x 33"
- Brown paper bag
- 100% cotton thread in matching color
- Assorted beads for embellishment

Cutting the Fabric

1. From the multi-color mandala fold tie-dyed fabric (A), cut:
   12 squares, each 3".

2. From the dark blue solid fabric (B), cut:
   2 strips, each 4½" x 20½".
   2 strips, each 4½" x 14½".
   2 bars, each 2" x 4½".
   6 circles, each 2½" diameter

3. From the light green solid fabric (C), cut:
   12 squares, each 3".
   2 strips, each 2½" x 10½".
   2 strips, each 2½" x 7½".

4. From the red solid fabric (D), cut:
   2 strips, each 3½" x 10½".
   2 strips, each 2½" x 7½".

5. From the multi-color spiral fold tie-dyed fabric (E), cut:
   2 strips, each 2½" x 10½".
   2 strips, each 2½" x 7½".

6. From the golden yellow drop painted fabric (F), cut:
   2 bars, each 2" x 4½".

7. From the brown paper bag, cut:
   6 circles, each 2½" (size of circular appliques).

Piecing the Quilt Top

Make Six Pinwheel Blocks:
Each pinwheel block is made from four half-square triangle blocks.

1. On the wrong side of the 12 light green (C) 3" squares, draw a pencil line on the diagonal from corner to corner.
2. Align them, right sides together, with 12 tie-dyed (A) 3" squares. Sew ¼" from the line on both sides, backstitching as you begin and end. Cut on the line to make two half-square triangle blocks. Repeat the process to make 24 in all. (Fig. 1)
3. With four half-square triangle blocks, make two rows of two each. Sew and press. You now have completed a pinwheel block. Make six in all. (Fig. 2 & 3)

Add Borders to Two Pinwheel Blocks:

1. Sew a 2" x 4½" blue bar on the right sides of two pinwheel blocks.
2. Sew a 2" x 4½" yellow bar on the left sides of the same two blocks. Press.
3. Position the blocks so the blue strip is at the left on block #1, and at the right on block #2.
4. Sew a 2½" x 7½" red strip to the top of block 1 and to the bottom of block 2. Press.
5. Sew a 2½" x 7½" strip of multi-color spiral fold tie dyed to the bottom of block 1 and the top of block 2. Press.
6. Sew a 2½" x 7½" strip of light green to the bottom of block 1 and the top of block 2. Press and set aside.

Make the Strip Sets:

1. Sew together:
   1 red strip, 3½" x 10½".
   1 light green strip, 2½" x 10½".
   1 multi-color tie-dyed strip, 2½" x 10½".
   Press. (Fig. 4)
2. Repeat with the remaining 10½" strips to make a second set. Press.

Assemble the Quilt Top:

1. Sew one strip set to the bottom of block 1. Sew the other strip set to the top of block 2. Press. (Fig. 5)
2. Using the photo as a guide for placement, align blocks and sew the center seam. Press.
3. Sew the 4½" x 14½" dark blue strips to the top and bottom.
4. Sew one of the remaining four pinwheel blocks to each end of the 4½" x 20½" dark blue strips. Press.
5. Sew the pinwheel strips to the sides of the quilt top. Press.
6. With the dark blue fabric circles and brown paper circles, make 6 circular appliques. See "Paper Bag Applique" on page 63 for instructions.
7. Sew the six circles on the red fabric strips, using the photo as a guide.

Fig. 1
Half-Square Triangle Block

Fig. 2
Pinwheel Block – Pieces Needed

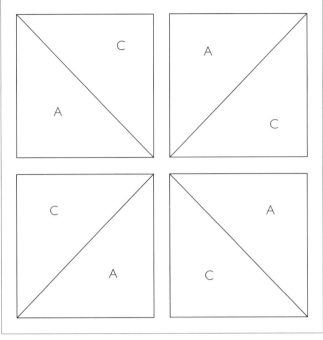

Fig. 3
Finished Block

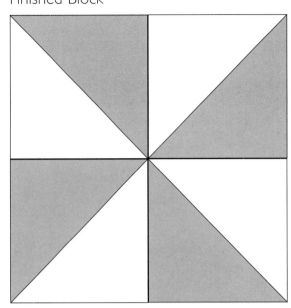

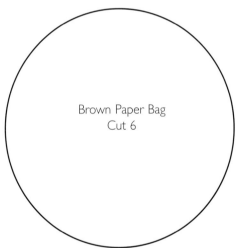

Brown Paper Bag
Cut 6

Fig. 4
Three-strip set
sew together

Fig. 5
Block #1

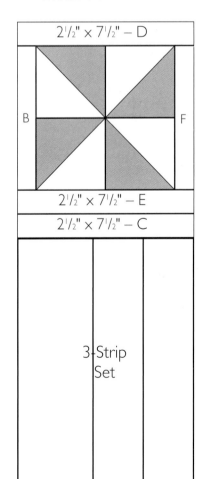

Constructing the Project

1. Make a quilt sandwich with the quilt top batting and backing, in that order. Make sure the top and batting are centered on the backing. Pin or needle baste it.
2. Beginning on one side, sew all around the edge of the quilt top to stabilize it, passing through all layers.
3. Quilt-in-the-ditch on all seams.
4. Quilt in other areas as desired, using the photo as a guide.
5. When you've finished quilting, trim the edges of the batting even with the edges of the quilt top.
6. Trim the backing fabric so it extends 1" all around the quilt top.
7. Fold in the edges of the backing fabric ½" toward the top on all sides, finger pressing as you go. Fold the remaining ½" of the backing fabric over the raw edges of the quilt top. Finger press and pin in place on all sides.
8. Blind stitch the binding in place.
9. Add beaded embellishments to the blue borders. See "Beading" in the "Artistic Embellishments" chapter for instructions about sewing beads. ❑

Shimmering Blocks & Bars Table Runner

This table runner has quarter-square triangle blocks and bar blocks of different sizes. It was created with six fabrics: two solids, one multi-color, two created with masking techniques, and one that was drop painted with metallic paint.

Swatches of dyed fabric used to make this project, pictured top to bottom:
A – Multi-color (peach, brown, aqua) hand dyed
B – Aqua and silver drop painted
C – Tan solid hand dyed
D – Brown and gray masked circles and diamonds
E – Brown and gray masked stripes
F – Dark brown solid hand dyed

Instructions begin on page 124.

Shimmering Blocks & Bars Table Runner

Pictured on page 122

Components

▧ Pieced top, 17¼" x 58"

▧ Batting, 17½" x 59"

▧ Backing fabric, 23½" x 65"

▧ 100% cotton thread of a matching color

Cutting the Fabric

1. From the multi-color hand-dyed fabric (A), cut:
   5 squares, each 7".
   6 bars, each 2" x 4½".
   4 strips, each 2½" x 12".
   5 bars, each 2½" x 6¼".

2. From the aqua and silver drop painted fabric (B), cut:
   5 squares, each 7".
   8 bars, each 2" x 4½".

3. From the tan solid fabric (C), cut:
   2 bars, each 2" x 4½".
   4 strips, each 2½" x 12".
   7 bars, each 2½" x 6¼".

4. From the brown and gray circles and diamonds fabric (D), cut:
   4 bars, each 2" x 4½".
   1 strip, 2½" x 12".
   2 bars, each 2½" x 6¼".

5. From the brown and gray striped fabric (E), cut:
   1 strip, 2½" x 12".
   2 bars, each 2½" x 6¼".

6. From the dark brown solid fabric (F), cut:
   4 bars, each 2" x 4½".
   5 strips, each 2½" x 12".
   8 bars, each 2½" x 6¼".

Piecing the Top

Create Nine Quarter-Square Triangle Blocks:
Pairs of multi-color 7" squares and drop-painted 7" squares were used.

1. On the back of the 7" drop-painted squares, draw a diagonal pencil corner to corner.
2. Align a multi-color square and a drop-painted square, right sides together, and sew ¼" from the line on both sides, back stitching as you begin and end. Cut on the line. Press the seam open. You now have half-square triangle blocks.
3. Draw another diagonal line on one of the pair of half-square triangle blocks perpendicular to the seam. Place them, right sides together, matching the seams. Sew ¼" from the line on both sides, back stitching as you begin and end. Cut on the line and press. You now have two quarter-square triangle blocks. (Fig. 1)
4. Repeat the process to make 10 in all. Set nine aside, and save the remaining one for another project.

Make the Strip Sets:

1. Make five strip sets, using groups of three 2½" x 11¾" strips in color combinations of your choice.
2. Make eight more strip sets, using three 2½" x 6¼" bars for each set in color combinations of your choice.
3. Make two strip set borders, each composed of twelve 2" x 4½" bars in assorted colors. Press and set aside. (Fig. 3)

Make the Panels:

1. Sew five panels with the 12" strip sets and five quarter-square triangle blocks. Place two with the strip set on the left side of the triangle block and three with the strip set on the right side of the triangle block. This is panel 1. (Fig. 4) Press.
2. Sew four panels with the 6¼" strip sets, placing a strip set on each side of each triangle block. This is panel 2. (Fig. 5) Press.

Assemble the Top:

1. Sew panels 1 and 2 together lengthwise, using the photo and Fig. 6 as a guide for placement. Press.
2. Sew a border strip of 2" x 4½" bars to each end. Press.

Constructing the Project

1. Make a quilt sandwich with the quilt top, batting, and backing, in that order. Make sure the quilt top and batting are centered on the backing. Pin or needle baste.
2. Beginning on one side, sew all around the edge of the quilt top to stabilize it, passing through all the layers.
3. Quilt-in-the-ditch along all the seams.
4. Trim the batting even with the edges of the quilt top.
5. Trim the backing so it extends 1" all around the quilt top.
6. Fold in the edges of the backing fabric ½" toward the top on all sides, finger pressing as you go. Fold the remaining ½" of the backing fabric over the raw edges of the quilt top. Finger press and pin in place on all sides.
7. Blind stitch the binding in place. ❏

Fig. 1
Quarter Square Triangle Block

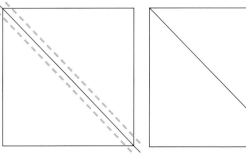

Place two solid squares right sides together. Stitch and cut on line drawn.

Press open. This is one half square triangle block.

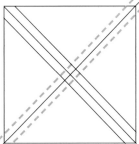

Place two half square triangle blocks right sides together. Stitch and cut on line drawn.

Press open. This will be a quarter square triangle block.

Fig. 2
Three-strip sets

sew together.

Fig. 3
Borders

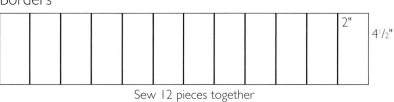

2"

4½"

Sew 12 pieces together

Fig. 4
Panel 1

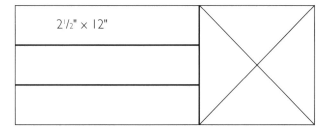

2½" × 12"

Fig. 5
Panel 2

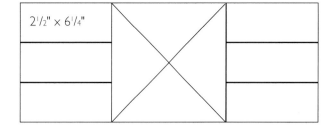

2½" × 6¼"

Fig. 6

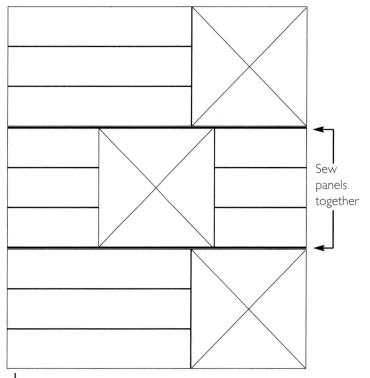

Sew panels together

Continued poisitioning Panel 1 in opposite direction each time.

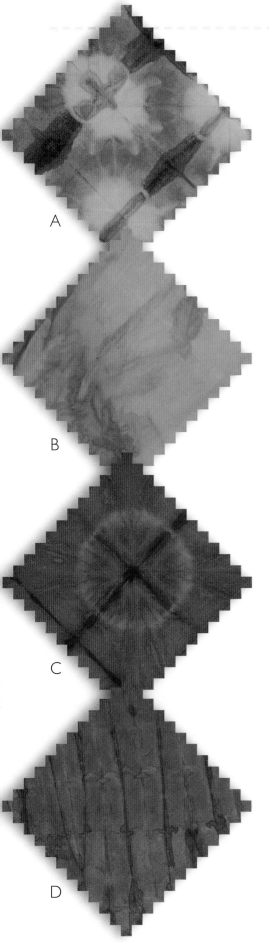

A

B

C

D

Quarter Square Nine Patch Quilt

This quilt is a combination of quarter-square triangle blocks and nine-patch blocks. It was created with four fabrics.

Pictured on page 126

Swatches of dyed fabric used to make this project, pictured top to bottom:
A - Turquoise and purple triangle fold tie dyed
B - Turquoise solid hand dyed
C - Red-violet triangle fold tie dyed
D - Purple random line fold tie dyed

Instructions begin on page 128

Quarter Square Nine Patch Quilt

Components

- Pieced top, 34½" square
- Batting, 35" square
- Backing fabric, 40" square
- 100% cotton thread of a matching color

Cutting the Fabric

1. From the turquoise and purple tie-dyed fabric (A), cut:
   4 squares, each 8".

2. From the turquoise solid fabric (B), cut:
   4 squares, each 8".
   4 strips, each 2¾" x 22".

3. From the red-violet tie-dyed fabric (C), cut:
   4 squares, each 8".
   7 strips, each 2¾" x 22".

4. From the purple tie-dyed (D), cut:
   4 squares, each 8".
   4 strips, each 2¾" x 22".
   1 piece, 40" square (for the backing).

Piecing the Top

Create 12 Quarter-Square Triangle Blocks:

1. On the wrong side of each turquoise solid square, draw a diagonal pencil line from corner to corner. Pair each with a purple tie-dyed square and place, right sides together. Align them and sew ¼" from the line on both sides, back stitching as you begin and end. Cut on the line and press. You will have six half-square triangle blocks.
2. Follow the same procedure with the red-violet tie-dyed squares and turquoise and purple tie-dyed squares to create six more half-square triangle blocks. Press the seams opposite those of the blocks in step 1.
3. Take the half-square triangle blocks you made in step 2 and draw a diagonal line perpendicular to the seam.
4. Pair each one with one from step 1, right sides together, with the diagonal seams in the same direction. Align them and sew ¼" from the drawn line on both sides. Cut, press, and set aside. You now have 12 quarter-square triangle blocks. (Fig. 1)

Create 13 Nine-Patch Blocks:

1. Make three-piece strip sets using the 2¾" x 22" strips:
   Strip Set A - Make 2. Red-violet, purple, red-violet (Fig. 2)
   Strip Set B - Make 1. Purple, turquoise, purple (Fig. 3)
   Strip Set C - Make 1. Red-violet, turquoise, red-violet (Fig. 4)
   Strip Set D - Make 1. Turquoise, red-violet, turquoise (Fig. 5)
2. Cut each strip set across the seams into 2¾" sections.
3. Create two different nine-patch blocks by sewing three sections together. Make seven blocks with A + B + A sections. Press. Make six blocks with C + D + C sections. Press.

Assemble the Top:

1. Lay the blocks out on the floor or on your design wall, in five horizontal rows with five blocks in each row. Alternate the Quarter Square Blocks and the Nine Patch Blocks.
2. Sew the horizontal rows together. Press them and lay them out in the same order.
3. Assemble the quilt top by sewing the horizontal rows together from top to bottom and press.

Constructing the Project

1. Make a quilt sandwich with the quilt top, batting, and backing, in that order. Make sure the quilt top and batting are centered on the backing. Pin or needle baste.
2. Beginning on one side, sew all around the edge of the quilt top to stabilize it, passing through all the layers.
3. Quilt-in-the-ditch along all the seams.
4. When the quilting is finished, trim the edges of the batting even with the edges of the quilt top.
5. Trim the backing to 1" all around the quilt top.
6. Fold in the edges of the backing fabric ½" toward the top on all sides, finger pressing as you go. Fold the remaining ½" of the backing fabric over the raw edges of the quilt top. Finger press and pin in place on all sides.
7. Blind stitch the binding in place. ❏

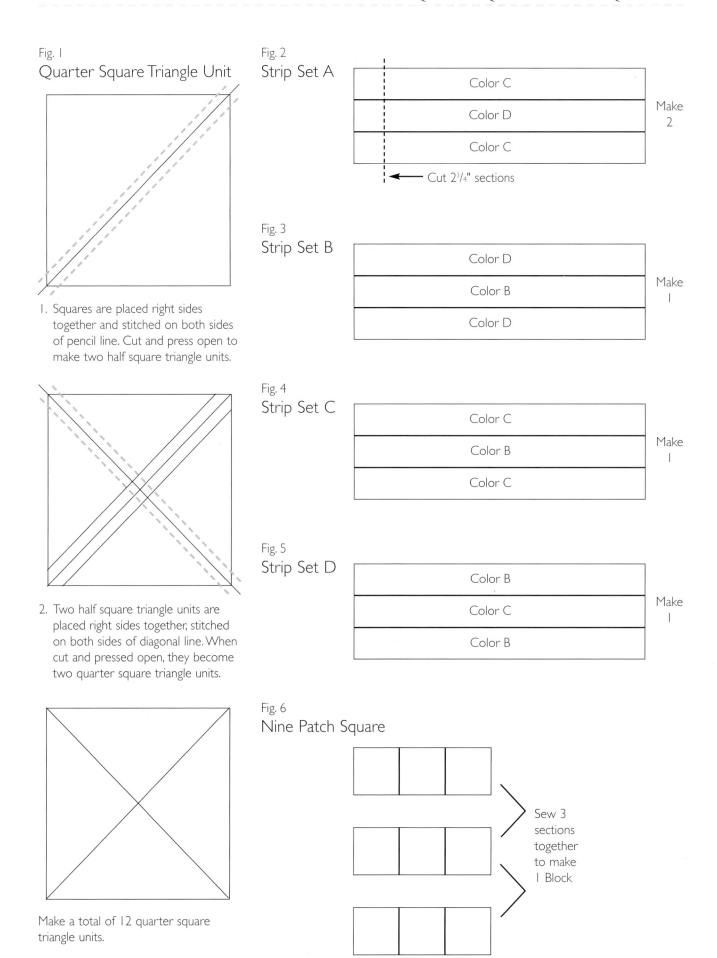

Fig. 1
Quarter Square Triangle Unit

1. Squares are placed right sides together and stitched on both sides of pencil line. Cut and press open to make two half square triangle units.

2. Two half square triangle units are placed right sides together, stitched on both sides of diagonal line. When cut and pressed open, they become two quarter square triangle units.

Make a total of 12 quarter square triangle units.

Fig. 2
Strip Set A

Color C
Color D
Color C

Make 2

← Cut 2³/₄" sections

Fig. 3
Strip Set B

Color D
Color B
Color D

Make 1

Fig. 4
Strip Set C

Color C
Color B
Color C

Make 1

Fig. 5
Strip Set D

Color B
Color C
Color B

Make 1

Fig. 6
Nine Patch Square

Sew 3 sections together to make 1 Block

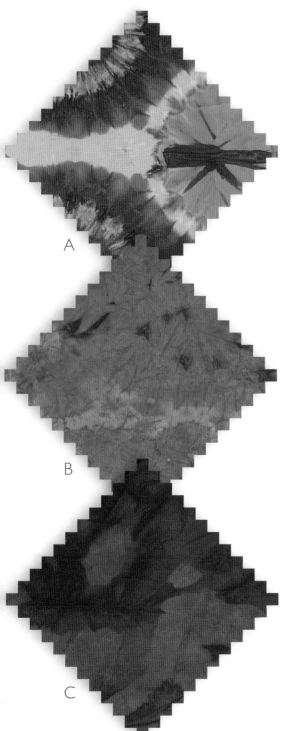

Shadow Block Quilt

This square quilt showcases the three primary colors. Composed of 25 blocks – 13 four-bar blocks and 12 shadow blocks, it was created with three fabrics – two solids and a mandala fold tie dyed.

Swatches of dyed fabric used to make this project, pictured top to bottom:
A – Multi-color (red, yellow, blue) mandala fold tie dyed
B – Blue soid hand dyed
C – Red solid hand dyed

Instructions begin on page 132.

Shadow Block Quilt

Pictured on page 130

Components

- Pieced top, 39" square
- Batting, 39½" square
- Backing fabric, 44" square
- 100% cotton thread in a matching color

Cutting the Fabric

1. From the multi-color tie-dyed fabric (A), cut:
   3 squares, each 9".

2. From the red solid fabric (B), cut:
   6 squares, each 8½"
   26 bars, each 2½" x 8½".
   1 piece, 44" square (for the backing)

3. From the blue solid fabric (C), cut:
   3 squares, each 9".
   26 bars, each 2½" x 8½".

Piecing the Top

Create 12 Shadow Blocks:

1. With a dark pencil, draw a diagonal line from corner to corner on the wrong side of the three multi-color squares. Pair each one with a blue square. Place them right sides together and align the edges. Sew ¼" from the line on both sides, back stitching as you begin and end.
2. Cut on the line and press to make six half-square triangle blocks.
3. Draw a diagonal pencil line corner to corner on the backs of the six red squares. Pair each one with a half-square triangle block, placing the drawn line perpendicular to the seam. With right sides together and the edges aligned, sew ¼" from the line on both sides, back stitching as you begin and end.
4. Cut on the line and press. When you are finished, you will have 12 shadow blocks.

Create 13 Four-Bar Blocks:

1. Take two red bars and two blue bars and make a block by alternately sewing them together. Press.
2. Continue this process until you have created 13 four-bar blocks.

Assemble the Top:

1. Lay out the squares on the floor or on your design wall, arranging them in five rows of five blocks each, alternating shadow blocks and four-bar blocks. Use the project photo and diagram as guides.
2. Sew each horizontal row together. Press them and lay them out in the same order.
3. Sew the horizontal rows together from top to bottom. Press.

Constructing the Project

1. Make a quilt sandwich with the quilt top, batting, and backing, in that order. Make sure the quilt top and batting are centered on the backing. Pin or needle baste.
2. Beginning on one side, sew all around the edge of the quilt top to stabilize it, passing through all the layers.
3. Quilt-in-the-ditch along all the seams.
4. When the quilting is finished, trim the edges of the batting even with the edges of the quilt top.
5. Trim the backing to 1" all around the quilt top.
6. Fold in the edges of the backing fabric ½" toward the top on all sides, finger pressing as you go. Fold the remaining ½" of the backing fabric over the raw edges of the quilt top. Finger press and pin in place on all sides.
7. Blind stitch the binding in place. ❑

Shadow Blocks

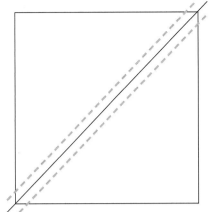

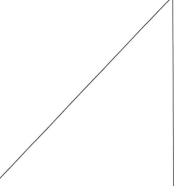

1. Place two squares right sides together and stitch. Cut on line drawn.

2. Press open. This makes two half square triangle blocks.

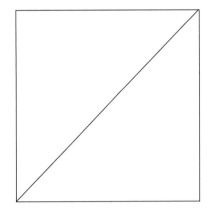

3. Use one solid square and one half square triangle block.

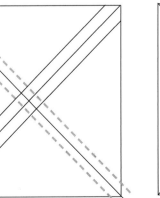

4. Place right sides together and stitch. Cut on line drawn and press open.

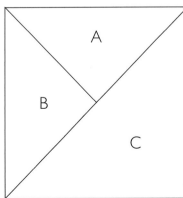

Finished Shadow Block

Four-Bar Block

B

C

B

C

Four bars stitched together creates one four-bar block.

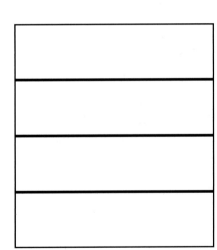

Finished Block

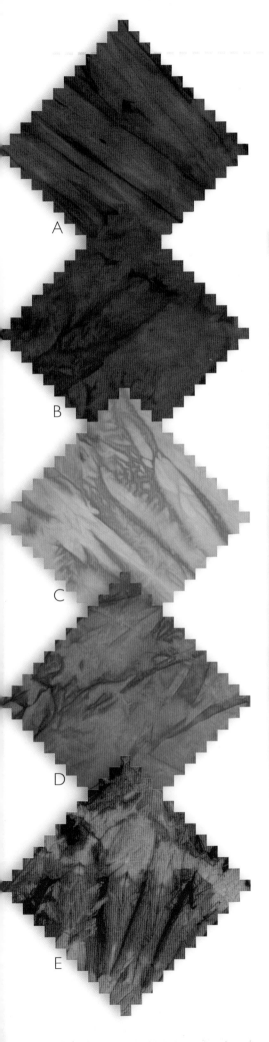

Come Inside Quilt

The Crooked Log Cabin technique takes center stage on this quilt using color to create feelings of depth and movement.

Swatches of dyed fabric used to make this project, pictured top to bottom:
A – Dark blue & purple random line fold tie dyed
B – Purple solid
C – Light blue solid
D – Aqua green solid
E – Red/Orange random line fold tie dyed

Instructions begin on page 136.

Come Inside Quilt

Pictured on page 134

Components
- Pieced top, 51" x 40"
- Batting, 51½" x 40½"
- Backing, 55" x 45" coordinating fabric
- 100% cotton thread in a matching color

Cutting the Fabrics

1. From the red/orange tie dye (E) cut:
   12 squares, each 2"
   2 strips, each 1½" x 30"
   2 strips, each 1½" x 41½"

2. From dark blue & purple tie dye (A)cut:
   15 strips, each 5" x 3"
   15 strips, each 12" x 3"
   15 wedges, 2" x 5½" x 2½"
   15 wedges, 2" x 5½" x 1½"

3. From purple solid (B) cut:
   15 strips, each 5" x 3"
   15 strips, each 12" x 3"
   15 wedges, 2" x 5½" x 2½"
   15 wedges, 2" x 5½" x 1½"

4. From light blue solid (C) cut:
   15 strips, each 5" x 3"
   15 strips, each 12" x 3"
   15 wedges, 2" x 5½" x 2½"
   15 wedges, 2" x 5½" x 1½"

5. From aqua green solid (D) cut:
   15 strips, each 5" x 3"
   15 strips, each 12" x 3"
   15 wedges, 2" x 5½" x 2½"
   15 wedges, 2" x 5½" x 1½"

Piecing the Crooked Log Cabin Blocks

1. Take a 2" red orange tie dye (E) square and align the left side with a 5" x 3" strip – the color of your choice. Sew a ¼" seam.
2. Trim the strip even with the square and press.
3. Pick another 5" x 3" strip (color of your choice) and place it right sides together with the top of the sewn unit at an angle. Sew a ¼" seam. Trim the strip even with the unit and press.
4. Continue adding strips around the square at different angles trimming as you go. Use the 12" x 3" strips on the longer edges. Sew 3 or 4 rows of strips around the Square. Trim to a 10" block size.
5. Create twelve 10" Crooked Log Cabin Blocks.

Assemble the Top

1. Create the border by sewing random colors of alternating 2½" and 2" wedges together, making two 40" x 5½" strips for the top and bottom border. Make two 42" x 5½" strips for the side borders.
2. Sew three Crooked Log Cabin Blocks together. You can rotate the blocks in different ways to create interest. Press.
3. Sew the rows together horizontally to create a 12 block panel. Press.
4. Sew the two 30" x 1½" red-orange tie-dyed strips to the top and bottom of the 12block panel.
5. Sew the two 41½" x 1½" red-orange tie-dyed strips to the sides of the 12-block panel. Press.
6. To complete the quilt top, sew two 42" x 5½" wedge strips to the sides of the panel. Press.
7. Finally, sew two 40" x 5½" wedge strips to the top and bottom of the 12-block panel. Press.

Constructing the Project

1. Make a quilt sandwich with the top, batting and backing, in that order. Pin or needle baste. Make sure the top and batting are centered on the backing.
2. Beginning on one side, sew all around the edge of the quilt top to stabilize it, passing through all the layers.
3. Quilt in-the-ditch along all the seams.
4. When the quilting is finished, trim back the batting to the edge of the quilt top.
5. Trim the backing to 1" all around.
6. To complete the quilt, fold over ½" of the backing fabric edge on all sides toward finger press as you go. Then fold the remaining ½" of the fabric binding over the raw edges of the quilt top. Finger press and pin it in place. Finish the binding by sewing it with a blind stitch. ❑

Border Section

Border Template

2"

2"

5½"

5½"

2½"

1½"

Crooked Log Cabin Block

E

30"
×
1½"

41½"
×
1½"

2" Square

E

5"×3" Strips

12"×3" Strips

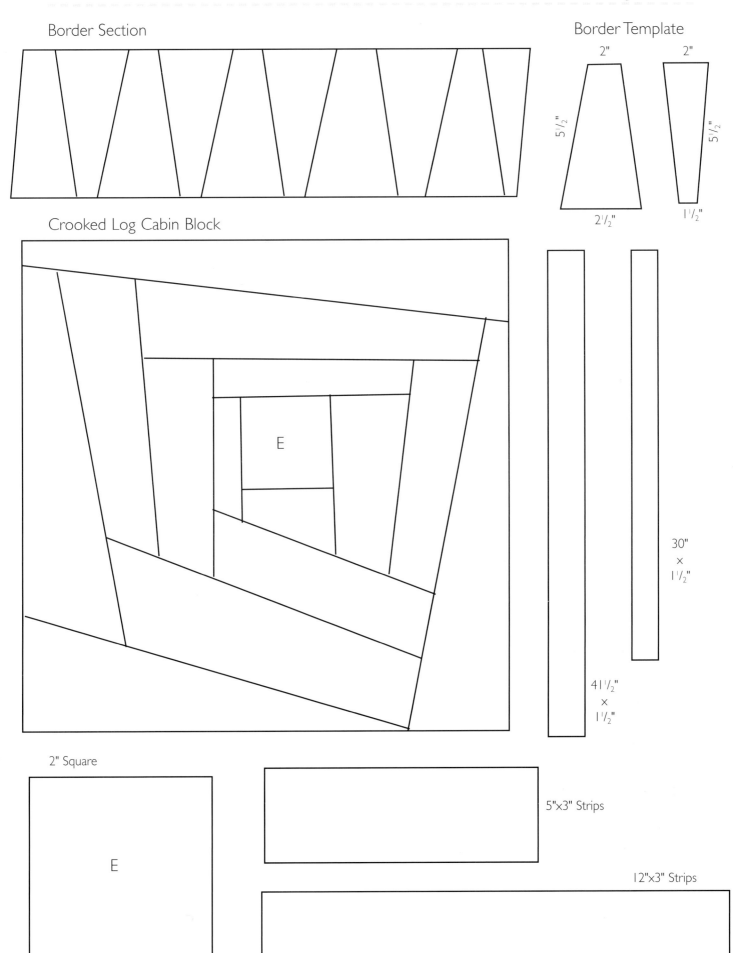

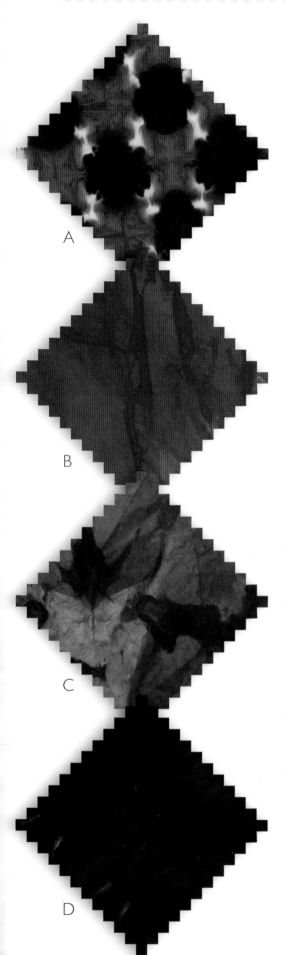

Quarter Squares & Bars Quilt

This pieced top is made from three sizes of quarter-square triangle blocks and three-bar blocks of different sides. The central medallion is embellished with beads. It was created with four dyed fabrics.

Swatches of dyed fabric used to make this project, pictured top to bottom:
A – Black, white & red checkerboard fold tie dyed
B – Red solid hand dyed
C – Gray solid hand dyed
D – Black solid hand dyed

Instructions begin on page 140

Quarter Squares & Bars Quilt

Pictured on page 138

Components

■ Pieced top, 21½" x 32"

■ Batting, 22" x 32½"

■ Backing fabric, 25" x 35"

■ 100% cotton thread of a matching color

■ Assorted beads to decorate center of quilt.

Cutting the Fabric

1. From the checkerboard tie-dyed fabric (A), cut:
   2 squares, each 7½".

2. From the red solid fabric (B), cut:
   2 squares, each 7½".
   4 squares, each 5".
   1 piece, 25" x 35" (for the backing)
   1 strip, 1½" x 20".

3. From the gray solid fabric (C), cut:
   1 square, 4½".
   4 strips, each 2½" x 22".
   1 strip, 1½" x 24".

4. From the black solid fabric (D), cut:
   1 square, 4½".
   4 squares, each 5".
   4 strips, each 2½" x 22".

Piecing the Blocks

Make the Quarter-Square Triangle Blocks:

Make 13 in all – four 6½", one 3½", and eight 4" (finished sizes).

1. Piece the quarter-square triangle blocks by first dividing all the squares into pairs. Take the lighter color of the pair and draw a diagonal line from corner to corner on the wrong side with a pencil. Take the other square of that pair and place the two squares right sides together with edges aligned.

2. Sew ¼" from the line on both sides, back stitching as you begin and end. Cut on the line and press with the seams open. (Fig. 1) With each pair of squares, you have made two half-square triangle blocks. (Fig. 2)

3. Draw another diagonal line on one of the pair of half-square triangle blocks perpendicular to the seam. Align the edges of the blocks, right sides together, with seams opposing each other.

4. Sew ¼" from the drawn line on both sides of the line, back stitching as you begin and end. Cut on the line and press.(Fig. 3) For each pair of half-square triangle blocks, you now have two quarter-square triangle blocks. (Fig. 4) Continue with all of the pairs of squares until completion. Set aside. Save one of the 3½" blocks for another project.

Quarter Square Triangle Blocks – 3¹⁄₂" block – Make 1

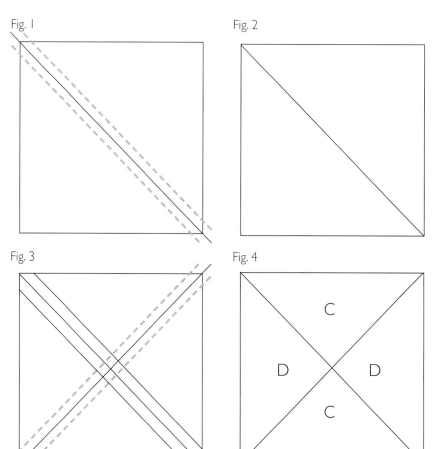

Fig. 1   Fig. 2

Fig. 3   Fig. 4

Make the Three-Strip Sets:

1. Create strip sets from the 2½" x 22" wide strips composed of one gray strip, one black strip, and one gray strip, in that order. (Fig. 7) Make two.

2. Cut them into four 2" sections, two 6½" sections, and two 8" sections.

Construct the Center Medallion Block:

1. Sew a 3½" section of the 1½" wide red strip on the top and bottom of the 3½" quarter-square triangle block. Press.

2. Sew a 5½" section of the 1½" wide red strip to the right and left sides. Press.

3. Sew a 5½" strip of the 1½" wide gray strip to the top and bottom of the block. Press.

4. Complete the medallion block by sewing a 6½" strip of 1½" wide gray to the right and left sides. Press. Trim, if necessary, to make a block 6½" square. (Fig. 8)

Assemble the Top:

1. Sew the 2" sections of the gray strip sets to each of the four 6½" quarter-square triangle blocks, using the photo and diagram as guides.

2. Sew one of these quarter-square units on each side of the 6½" strip set units. (This will create two rows.) Press.

3. Create the middle row by sewing the 8" strip set units to the sides of the center medallion. Press.

4. Sew the rows together with the center medallion row in the middle. Press. (Fig. 9)

5. Sew a 2½" x 22" black strip on each side of the pieced top. Press and trim. (Fig. 9)

6. Sew the remaining 2½" x 22" black strips to the top and bottom.

Continued on next page

Fig. 5
6½" blocks – Make 4

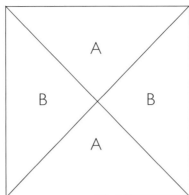

Fig. 6
4" blocks – Make 8

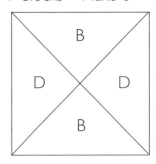

Fig. 7
Three-strip sets – Make 2

three strips
sewn together

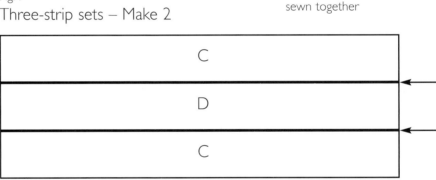

Fig. 8
Medallion Block

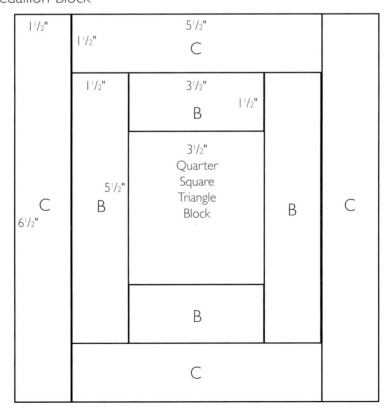

Quarter Squares & Bars Quilt, continued

7. Make the top and bottom borders by sewing 2½" x 4" gray bars to the 4" quarter-square triangle blocks, alternating the gray bars (five in each row) and quarter-square triangle blocks (four in each row). Press. (Fig. 10)

8. Sew the border strips to the top and bottom of the quilt top. Press and trim, if necessary.

Constructing the Project

1. Make a quilt sandwich with the quilt top batting and backing, in that order. Make sure the top and batting are centered on the backing. Pin or needle baste it.

2. Beginning on one side, sew all around the edge of the quilt top to stabilize it, passing through all layers.

3. Quilt-in-the-ditch on all seams.

4. When you've finished quilting, trim the edges of the batting even with the edges of the quilt top.

5. Trim the backing fabric so it extends 1" all around the quilt top.

6. Fold in the edges of the backing fabric ½" toward the top on all sides, finger pressing as you go. Fold the remaining ½" of the backing fabric over the raw edges of the quilt top. Finger press and pin in place on all sides.

7. Blind stitch the binding in place.

8. Add beaded embellishments to the center medallion. See "Beading" in the "Artistic Embellishments" chapter for instructions about sewing beads. ❏

Fig. 9

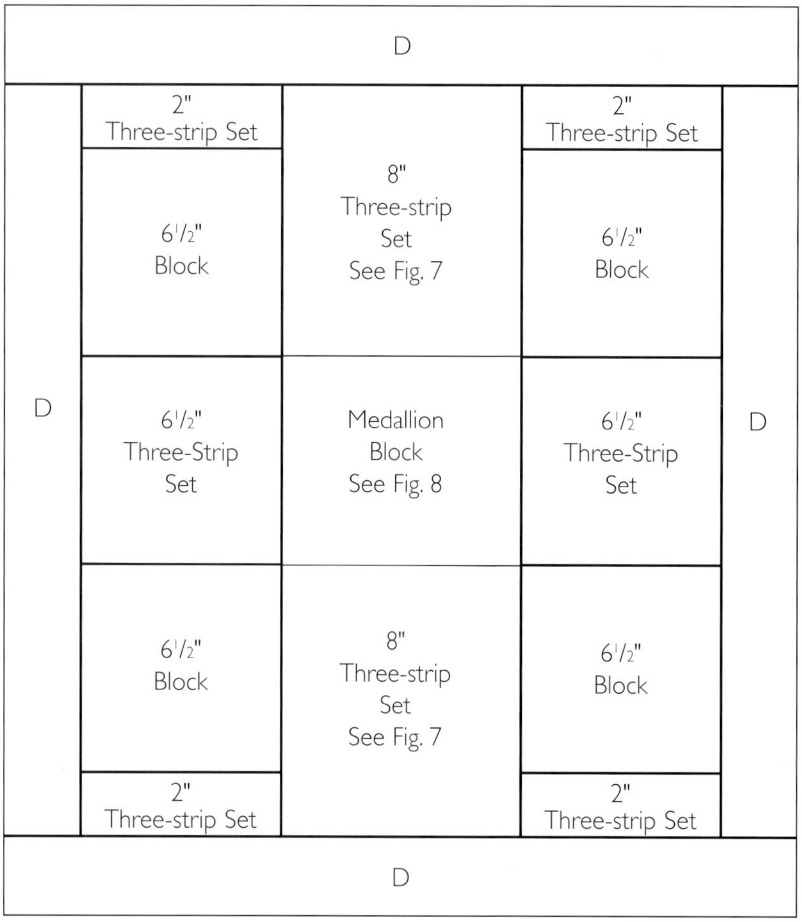

	D		
	2" Three-strip Set		2" Three-strip Set
	6½" Block	8" Three-strip Set See Fig. 7	6½" Block
D	6½" Three-Strip Set	Medallion Block See Fig. 8	6½" Three-Strip Set	D
	6½" Block	8" Three-strip Set See Fig. 7	6½" Block
	2" Three-strip Set		2" Three-strip Set
	D		

Fig. 10

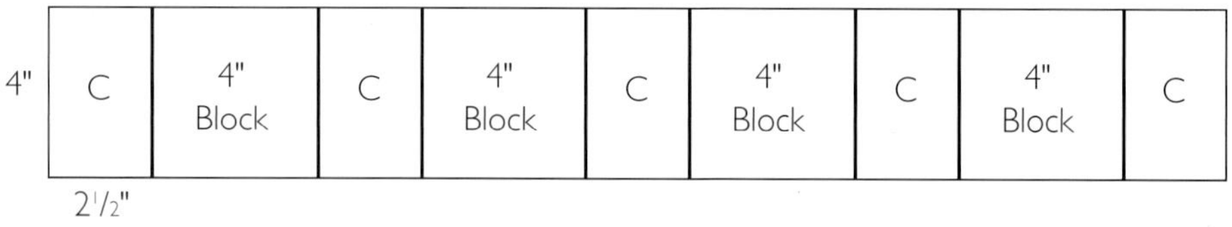

4"	C	4" Block	C	4" Block	C	4" Block	C	4" Block	C

2½"

Metric Conversion Chart

Inches to Millimeters and Centimeters

Inches	MM	CM	Inches	MM	CM
1/8	3	.3	2	51	5.1
1/4	6	.6	3	76	7.6
3/8	10	1.0	4	102	10.2
1/2	13	1.3	5	127	12.7
5/8	16	1.6	6	152	15.2
3/4	19	1.9	7	178	17.8
7/8	22	2.2	8	203	20.3
1	25	2.5	9	229	22.9
1-1/4	32	3.2	10	254	25.4
1-1/2	38	3.8	11	279	27.9
1-3/4	44	4.4	12	305	30.5

Yards to Meters

Yards	Meters	Yards	Meters
1/8	.11	3	2.74
1/4	.23	4	3.66
3/8	.34	5	4.57
1/2	.46	6	5.49
5/8	.57	7	6.40
3/4	.69	8	7.32
7/8	.80	9	8.23
1	.91	10	9.14
2	1.83		

Index

A
Air brush paint 16
Applique
  interfacing 62
  paper bag 63
Appliqued Circles Quilt 118
Artist 5

B
Bags, plastic zip-top 17
Basin, plastic 17
Basting 53
Batting 50, 70, 72, 75, 85, 88, 92, 96, 100, 104, 106, 112, 117, 120, 124, 128, 132, 136, 140
Beaded Blues Bookmark 80
Beading 60
Beads 58, 60, 72, 75, 81, 88, 104, 117, 120, 140
Binding 54
Black, examples 42
Block quilt 86
Blue Blossoms Quilt 110
Blue, examples 32, 33
Bookmark 80
Brown, examples 43
Button 58

C
Cardboard 50
Chalk 60
  tailor's 50
Color Wheel Checkerboard Drop Painted Quilt 115
Color
  complementary 14
  contrast 14
  families 28
  hue 14
  learning about 12
  value 14
  wheel 13
Colored pencil(s) 50
Come Inside Quilt 134
Contrast, color 14
Cord, braided 72

D
Drip Painting 44
Dyeing
  drip painting 44
  fabrics for 16
  folded fabric 20
  masking method 46
  method 15

preparation 18
supplies 16
terminology 47

E
Embellished Bars Pin Cushion 74
Embellishments, artistic 57
Embroidery floss 50, 58, 117
Eye glass case 72

F
Fabric(s) 58, 62, 63, 72
  backing 17, 70, 72, 75, 79, 81, 85, 88, 92, 96, 100, 104, 106, 112, 117, 120, 124, 128, 132, 136, 140
  cutting 51
  flower stems 112
  for dyeing 16
  leaf shapes 112
  pieced 88, 92, 96, 100, 104, 108, 112, 117, 120, 124, 128, 132, 136, 140
  pieced block 70, 72, 75, 79, 85
  pieced flower pot 112
  pieced strip 81
  piecing 51, 52
  prepare 18
  pressing 52

Continued on next page

Index, continued

Flannel 81
Folds
  checkerboard 24
  concentric circles 26
  envelope 24
  fan 22
  fan variation 23
  mandala tie 27
  multiple circle 27
  random circles 27
  random line 25
  spiral 26
  triangle 25
Freezer paper 17, 46
Fuchsia, examples 30, 31

G
Gloves, protective 17
Golden yellows, examples 36, 37
Graph paper 50
Green, examples 38, 39

H
Hanging quilts 56
Hills & Valleys Table Topper 91
Hot pads 68
House Top Pillow 98

I
Interfacing 62, 112
  applique 62
Introduction 8
Iron 17, 50

J
Jazzy Checkerboard Quilt 102

M
Masking 46
Mat 84
Maverick Block Quilt 86
Muslin 96, 100

N
Needle(s) 60, 62
  hand sewing 50, 63
  machine sewing 50
Newsprint 17
Nine Patch Pot Holders 78

O
Orange, examples 34, 35

P
Paint, air brush 16
Painting, drip 44
Paper bag 63, 120
Paper bag applique 63
Paper plates 17
Paper towels 17
Pearl cotton 50
Pencil 60, 62
Pigment, prepare 18
Pillow 94, 98
Pin cushion 74
Pin(s)
  cushion 50
  safety 50
  straight 50, 62, 63
Pot holders 78
Preparation, dyeing 18
Projects 66
Purples, examples 40, 41

Q
Quarter Square Nine Patch Quilt 126
Quarter Squares & Bars Quilt 130
Quilt 86, 102, 106, 110, 115, 118,
  126, 130, 134, 138
  assembling 53
Quilting
  basics 48
  supplies 49
  techniques 51
  terminology 64

R
Rack, drying 17
Rail Fence Quilt 106
Red, examples 28, 29
Rotary cutting tool 49
Rotary ruler 50
Rubber bands 17

S
Scissors 17, 49, 58, 62, 63
Seam ripper 50
Shadow Block Quilt 130
Shell 75, 100
Shimmering Blocks & Bars Table
  Runner 122
Sky & Meadow Floor Pillow 94
Solids, dyeing 18
Squeeze bottles 17
Stenciling 46
Stuffing 75, 96, 100
Supplies
  dyeing 16
  quilting 49

T
Table runner 122
Table topper 91
Techniques, basic quilting 51
Template, plastic 50
Terminology 47, 64
Thimble 50
Thread
  cotton 50, 60, 63, 70, 75, 79, 81,
    85, 88, 92, 96, 100, 104, 106,
    112, 117, 120, 124, 128, 132,
    136, 140
  metallic 50
  monofilament nylon 50
  quilting 50
  sewing 50, 58, 62
Tiny Squares Eye Glass Case 72
Triangles & Bars Hot or Cold Mat 84

X
X Marks the Spot Hot Pads 68

Y
Yo-yos 58, 112